India's Legendary
EAST COAST

India's Legendary
EAST COAST

P.K. De

NIYOGI
BOOKS

Published by

NIYOGI BOOKS

D-78, Okhla Industrial Area, Phase-I
New Delhi-110 020, India
Tel: 91-11-26816301, 49327000
Fax: 91-11-26810483, 26813830
email: niyogibooks@gmail.com
www.niyogibooks.com

Text and photographs ©: P.K. De
Editor: Nandita Jaishankar/Niyogi Books
Design: Write Media

ISBN: 978-93-81523-12-4
Year of Publication: 2012

Printed at: Niyogi Offset Pvt. Ltd., New Delhi, India

Dedicated to
all footloose beachcombers

THE EASTERN COASTLINE OF INDIA

BANGLADESH

WEST BENGAL

Kolkata

Gosaba

Sunderbans

Digha

Baleshwar

ODISHA

Cuttack

Bhubaneshwar

Paradip

Puri

Ganjam

Gopalpur

Hyderabad

Vizag

ANDHRA PRADESH

Kakinada Port

Yanam

Narsapur

Machlipatnam

Chirala

Nellore

BAY OF BENGAL

Chennai

Kanchipuram

Puducherry

Cuddalore

Chidambaram

TAMIL NADU

Karaikal

Nagore

Nagapattinam

Thiruvarur

Velankanni

Rameshwaram

Fisheries Coast

Mandapam

Tuticorin

Tiruchendur

Kanyakumari

SRI LANKA

INDIAN OCEAN

Map not to scale

Contents

An agrarian coastal plain in Odisha

Preface

Discovering the East Coast of India

My initiation to explore the East Coast of India was solemnised about fifty years ago when, as Photo-officer to the Department of Tourism of the Government of India, I was assigned to portray and present the great Sun Temple of Konark in Odisha (Orissa) through lively photographs that would serve as posters as well as tourist literature. This new department, under the Ministry of Tourism and Civil Aviation, was then located within several dingy hutments called the Taj Barracks, off Connaught Place in New Delhi where today stands a big shopping complex and the multi-storeyed Tel Bhavan. At the time, the Department of Tourism was headed by Sri Som Nath Chib, a far-sighted man with great vision who was later acclaimed as the 'Father of Indian Tourism'.

In those days, tourism in the country meant attracting travellers from abroad who would bring with them plenty of foreign exchange. Those who were at the helm of the tourism industry had the notion that there were only a few places in the country worth being shown to foreigners, namely, affluent American tourists who would feel happy to 'do India' in the shortest possible time. Hence only a few places in the North, not too far from Delhi, were the chosen destinations for quick sightseeing. Usually the itinerary would cover a few days of touring the Kashmir Valley followed by a compact air-tour package of another few days visiting the triangle of Agra-Khajuraho-Varanasi. Tourism in the heritage-rich South or in the little known lively East lacked the essential infrastructure needed for quick and comfortable sightseeing. Visits to the East or South were, therefore, very exclusive and limited to only those few serious travellers whose sojourn was for a longer duration, and who would not mind roughing it out in the process of exploring and gaining an intimate idea of a new, exotic country.

With his far-sighted outlook as well as realistic conception, Som Nath Chib brought about revolutionary changes in the development of tourism in India. Under his guidance scenic, historic and heritage sites across the country were identified, explored and brought under the fold of the Department of Tourism at the centre and the state level. The Department of Tourism emerged as an important autonomous body and was re-named the India Tourism Development Corporation (ITDC) with a branch in every state. The newly formed ITDC not only catered to the needs of foreign travellers but would also guide and encourage domestic tourists. Accordingly, various state tourism departments were created, refurbished and upgraded with the necessary infrastructures to keep the tourism industry flourishing all year round and in each state. A monthly journal *Traveller in India* was published in Delhi while millions of posters, illustrated pamphlets, handouts and tourist information bulletins were printed for distribution to potential tourists. All these publications needed attractive pictures as illustrations.

To start my mission, I selected the ancient and hallowed grounds of the Konark Sun Temple in coastal Odisha on the Bay of Bengal. I landed there on a late summer afternoon travelling by a ramshackle public bus all the way from the state capital Bhubaneshwar. For any visitor today it would be impossible to get an idea as to what sort of a place today's crowded Konark was about fifty years ago. I still vividly recollect my first night at Konark which was then a tiny nondescript place, less than a village and totally devoid of human habitation after dark. During the day, only one or two isolated groups of pilgrims or some stray visitor like me would drop in to have a cursory look at the Sun Temple on the way to the holy shrine of Lord Jagannath at Puri. Nobody would spend a night at Konark, in fact there was no place to stay! Fortunately for me, on government duty, there was some shelter—a small PWD *dak* bungalow in the midst of an open field close to the temple. With a kerosene lamp in hand, the *chowkidar* (watchman) of the bungalow welcomed me in the two-room tenement that was empty except for a shaky *charpoy* (cot) and a small rusty iron table. Hardly before I could settle myself in these new surroundings, he advised me to hurry up for my meal, as the only *dhaba* (roadside eatery) of the place was about to close down as the sun had already set. There was no electricity in Konark

One of the twenty-four wheels of the Sun Temple in Konark, Odisha

in those days, and it became dark all around soon after sunset. Through the darkness, the shadowy silhouette of the derelict gigantic temple loomed large, faintly lit by the fading glow of the evening sky. And so, at seven pm, I finished my hearty dinner—a simple meal of steaming hot rice and fresh sea fish cooked in a tasty soup. As soon as I returned to the bungalow, the *chowkidar* wished me good night promising to come again in the morning, as he, along with the cooks at the *dhaba*, had to return home in their village a kilometre away. After his hurried departure I was left all alone in a profound darkness with only a dim lantern casting eerie shadows to keep me company. It was a bizarre feeling that kept me awake till the late hours of the night, listening all the while to the relentless, crashing waves from the sea not too far away. At dawn the next day I walked down a mile to the coast for my first ever rendezvous with the sea. The scenic grandeur of the

A sculpture of a stone horse at the Konark Sun Temple

Bay of Bengal at sunrise mesmerised me for a long time rewarding me well for all the hardships I had undertaken to be there. Since that day I developed an avid fascination for the sea which grew so great that I would always respond to its beckoning at any opportunity. On this occasion from Konark, trailing the coastal route I went up to Gopalpur, visiting Jagannath Puri and Lake Chilka along the way. On later opportunities, other than the Odisha coast, I explored the Sunderbans in coastal Bengal and the beach routes in

Konark Beach at sunset

Andhra Pradesh and in Tamil Nadu on several occasions. Of my other visits to Konark in the years that followed, the most memorable occasion came on 16 February 1980—on this day, the Konark Sun Temple happened to be under the trajectory of the total solar eclipse. The photographs that I took of this rare event were carried on the front page of all the leading dailies and were also included later in the *Encyclopaedia Britannica*.

At the end of my career I had taken to photojournalism and continued my photo-travels as well as writing travelogues on behalf of several dailies and periodicals. By then visiting places on the eastern coast of India had become my passion; in the process of frequent visits, I became familiar with numerous enthralling tales woven with the strands of beliefs and myths associated with the magnificent East Coast. Almost all these legends are imbued with some kind of divine fragrance and would relate to various attributes of the gods and incarnations. These mythological stories also reveal the eternal and inseparable cultural bond existing between the north and the south of our great ancient country. In the present narrative I have cited only such tales and the legends which are backed both by the scriptures as well as by history.

Women at Marina Beach, Chennai

Introduction

Coastal havens are the meeting places of seafaring people from different lands; like open windows, the coast displays glimpses of the inland country to mariners as well as to the world outside. The ambience of a country surrounded by the sea often permeates its littoral regions as well. A shoreline that shelters many ports and harbours also helps in promoting interactions between nations diffusing spontaneous exchange of ideas, beliefs, craft-skills and culture. The Indian mainland has an extensive coastline of 6,100 kilometres east to west, touching the Cape Comorin (Kanyakumari), the southernmost tip of the subcontinent. Originating in the east from Bengal's Gangetic delta, the coastline encompasses the great peninsula trailing up to the creek of the Arabian Sea near the Rann of Kutch in Gujarat, close to the mouth of the Indus River. This enormous periphery covers eight major Indian states, almost half the total landmass of the entire country. Rich in history and diverse cultural heritage of its vast hinterland, India's coastline presents a remarkable image of itself which is unparalleled in the world.

The eastern wing of the coast, spread over nearly 2,800 kilometres, begins from the delta of the Ganga on the Bay of Bengal and extends up to Land's End at Kanyakumari in the south. However, its much splendoured history together with the kaleidoscopic images of the various places that it traverses, far outshines the colours of the remaining coastal region. The East Coast has several rare as well as distinctive features of its own. It may well be assumed that this is veritably the sacred coast of this great country, where lie numerous holy places of pilgrimage, such as the Ganga Sagar, Puri, Visakhapatnam, Puducherry (Pondicherry), Chidambaram, Rameshwaram, Nagore, Velankanni, Kanyakumari and others, belonging to different faiths and being respected equally by all. It is also the coast of confluences as the principal rivers of India—the Ganga, the Mahanadi, Godavari, Krishna and Kaveri, all being considered holy, flow into the Bay of Bengal. This is again, the glorious historic coast from where Indian civilisation as well as Buddhism spread to Sri Lanka, Burma and the countries of Southeast Asia. The eastern coast also happens to be the coast of myths and legends supported by the ancient scriptures and history of the land. Every bend of the eastern shoreline, each solitary cove on the Bay of Bengal has its own unique account, interesting chronicles and favourite folktales. These anecdotes, often linked to the surrounding hinterland as well, enliven the cultural heritage of India as a whole. The accounts of India's coastline are thus closely interwoven with the many strands of legends of the country's hinterland.

The long stretch of the East Coast from coastal West Bengal till Land's End at Kanyakumari may be traversed by land routes trailing the extensive shoreline, though to cover this great distance by road all the way may be quite tough in places if not impossible. In fact, there is a national plan to construct an all-weather coastal route along the entire shoreline of India that would connect all the isolated strips of the beach roads. Presently, the two National Highways 45 and 45A and branch routes cover most of the stretch lying across the states of Odisha, Andhra Pradesh and Tamil Nadu.

Velankanni Church, Tamil Nadu

The East Coast Road (ECR) of Tamil Nadu is a two-lane express highway built along the coast of the Bay of Bengal; currently, it connects the metro-city Chennai with the city of Ramanad, about 500 kilometres south and is expected to be extended further up to Thoothukodi (Tuticorin) and beyond. The span between Baleshwar and Gopalpur via Konark, Puri and Lake Chilka offers an enchanting drive along the coastal road amidst scenic natural beauty; the East Coast route is further extended to Vizag (Visakhapatnam) through the picturesque landscape and beaches around Bheemunipatnam in Andhra Pradesh. Another excellent coastal route is the 166 kilometre-stretch from Chennai to Puducherry (Pondicherry), enjoyable traversing all the way through many interesting places; the smooth and wide open road narrows thereafter winding through what may be called, a 'secular zone', the erstwhile French town of Karaikal where Hindu temples are seen at almost every corner, then the Muslim Dargah of Hazrat Sayed Shah Abdul Hameed at Nagore, and finally the Catholic Church at Velankanni dedicated to Mother Mary. Proceeding further ahead, Kodikkarai (Point Calimere) is reached where the Fisheries Coast begins. This area is almost devoid of any major habitation other than fishing villages. The uneven winding road that is locally known as the infamous 'Smugglers Route' thereafter becomes narrow and hazardous until it merges with the National Highway 210 at Ramanathapuram.

This long expanse of India's shore from the Sunderbans up to Kanyakumari contains the turbulent waters of the Bay of Bengal that wash the eastern coastal region. It defines the landscapes, demarcates the state boundaries and depicts the way of life of the people living there for generations. From Bengal to Odisha, Andhra Pradesh to Tamil Nadu, there will be variations in language, custom and cultural patterns; but the states are all linked together by one common coastline which is legendary as well as sacred. All the adjoining habitations on the coastal region irrespective of the individual state boundary share many commonalities regardless of their varied differences. Barring some minor exceptions, the physical features or landscape of the coast in general are not very different—dramatic views of the infinite golden sandy beach continuously trailing alongside an azure expanse of the sea and the dazzling breakers in its fold. The shoreline curving

Women in the paddy fields, Andhra Pradesh

on and on recedes away intermingling with the distant horizon often dotted with fishermen's villages or is hidden at times behind a rocky promontory jutting out of the sea. The rural plains forming the hinterland present a grand view of the vast, green agrarian landscape, sometimes with the backdrop of the distant low lying hills of the Eastern Ghats. Variations in the scene are interposed by a few charming lakes or lagoons as well as by the bewildering array of exotic flora and fauna in the mangrove forested deltas of great rivers. Though rice is the staple produce in the coastal plains, for a large number of people thriving on the shore, the principal livelihood is fishing on the turbulent seas, riding their catamarans as has been the practice since the dawn of civilisation. Long before the Europeans could reach Southeast Asia, generations of these coastal people were daring seafarers and traders.

Like the spice coast of Malabar in the West, the historic Coromandel Coast—the prime extent of the eastern coastline—was long known to the outside world as the treasure house of coveted Indian goods: cotton and silk textiles, the finest pearls, exotic perfumes and shining bronzes besides various aromatic spices. Coins excavated at different places on the east coast establish the fact that Rome, Greece, Egypt, China and the Arab world have had trading relations with India since time immemorial. For centuries, until the Portuguese Vasco da Gama reached India after a long, circuitous voyage around the continent of Africa, the west coast of India remained the exclusive domain of the seafaring Arab merchants; they would trade with India and sail their dhows across the seas loaded with precious Indian goods meant for the hungry European market.

With the arrival of the Portuguese in 1498 the Arab monopoly received a setback and long lasting feuds started on the western coast of India for wresting the supremacy over trading rights. While the Portuguese remained engaged in fencing with the Arabs and colonising the Malabar Coast, other emerging European maritime powers had been settling themselves in the peaceful and encouraging atmosphere of the Eastern Coast. The Portuguese somehow managed to establish themselves only at a few posts on the east though not for too long; notable among these places were Hooghly and Chittagong, both tranquil quarters in Bengal.

The people living on the coast girdling the Bay of Bengal were also acclaimed maritime traders. *Saudagars* (merchants) of Bengal and Odisha were early notable seafarers since Mauryan times. Later, the Pallava and the Chola emperors of the south were also great promoters of commerce; they used to send merchant navies across the seas to Burma, Ceylon and the countries in Southeast Asia.

From the delta of the Ganga south of Bengal till Kanyakumari, numerous ports and harbours came up, flourished and faded with the passage of time, all within a span of 1,000 years. From other lands, too, ships would arrive loaded with gold and other expensive minerals for trading at these ports as well as for transit en route to the Far East. Chinese accounts say that the Chola ports were veritably great emporia, overflowing with varied precious commodities like ivory, rhinoceros horns, ebony, amber, gemstones, pearls, and prized perfumes, in addition to aromatic spices and exotic textiles. Other than trading, the seafarers would also exchange knowledge, tales and myths, traditions and skills. Later, the advent of European powers and their missionaries in the sixteenth to seventeenth century further enhanced the process of influencing Indian culture and religions. The flavours of those ancient days still linger on, drifting across time to enrich India's history and heritage.

Demarcated in history as the legendary Coromandel Coast, a large extent of the East Coast of India once spanned the great distance from Ganjam in the south of Odisha to Point Calimere (Kodikkarai) in Tamil Nadu. Those were the golden days (tenth to fourteenth century AD) of the mighty Chola kings reigning in South India, who also ruled Andhra Pradesh and the kingdom of Kalinga (Odisha) for many years. In fact, the term Coromandel is actually a distortion of the word 'Cholamandalam' meaning the royal domain of the Chola dynasty. The great Cholas are believed to have been amongst the early sponsors of seafaring vessels

Revellers taking a dip at the beach in Puri

that set out across the Bay of Bengal carrying Indian merchandise to markets abroad. Much later, when the British arrived to trade, they anglicised the name Cholamandalam to Coromandel. The British East India Company afterwards also altered the perimeter of the Coromandel Coast redefining its extension from port Chirala on the Krishna Delta in present day Andhra Pradesh, up to Land's End at Kanyakumari in south Tamil Nadu. However, the coastal stretch from Point Calimere further down is better known as the Fisheries Coast, as initially named by the Portuguese.

Sunset on the Hooghly River

West Bengal

On its easternmost extremity, coastal India begins from the mouth of the great Ganga River south of Bengal. The alluvial plains of Bengal (Vanga or Banga) find mention in the holy Puranas, in the great epic *Mahabharata* as well as in Ptolemy's (Claudius Ptolemaeus, c. AD 2) geography; also mentioned in history as the country of Gowd or the Samo-tat (Coastal Plain), Bengal has a long antiquated history dating back to the Aryan invasions of India. In circa AD 300 Bengal was included in the Mauryan Empire. Seafaring Bengali traders used to sail across the seas to Sri Lanka, Bali and Sumatra in Southeast Asia. Greek, Persian and Chinese traders too used to visit Bengal either by the land route or by the sea, reaching the ports of Tamralipta and Saptagram.

Vaishnav shrine in Tamralipta

The coastline south of Bengal is fragmented into numerous islands forming the great Gangetic delta, the world's largest delta, much of which falls inside the adjoining country of Bangladesh that was once a part of India. Here the Hooghly River inundates a vast expanse of a 4,263 square kilometre dense forest zone, the Sunderbans. Possibly named after the rare and valuable Sundari trees, the Sunderbans is world famous for its vast domain of mangrove forests, the largest in the world as well as for abounding in a wide variety of exotic fauna of which the most famous is the Royal Bengal tiger.

The Sunderbans is a confusing labyrinth of wide rivers, creeks and numerous narrow waterways dotted with many islands of thick mangrove swamps. In close contact with the sea, mangrove trees thrive best in saline water protecting the land from erosion against cyclones and tidal waves. The trees are small and bushy with shiny leaves, sharp, elongated and mostly erect aerial roots which serve as breathers and provide anchorage during the flooding high tides that come in twice daily. When the water recedes, the widespread low lands become visible with millions of sharp spikes of aerial roots, locally called *shulo*, all of them pointing skywards. Just fifty-four of such 102 islands are inhabited, the rest are impenetrable marshy

A boat stuck in the mud after the floods in the Sunderbans

Contrary to popular belief, the Bengal tigers inhabiting the Sunderbans are neither the largest nor the strongest of their kind. In reality, they are the same striped animals of the species *Panthera tigris*, living in the other jungles of the country. However, they are decidedly the dominating king of the forest because of their cunning and ferocity and their daring and prowess in swimming across wide rivers. Tigers are also dreaded in the

A tiger hunting fish in the Sunderbans and (right) swimming across the Matla River

Sunderbans because several of them have turned into maneaters. In one of my river trips through the Sunderbans, I chanced upon a tiger that was swimming across the wide and turbulent Matla River. In spite of our motor boat speeding up we failed to catch up with the beast before it landed on shore and disappeared into the dense forest.

forests teeming with an immense variety of avian, reptilian and aquatic life. Playing a crucial ecological role, mangroves of the Sunderbans protect the environment from the adverse effects of global warming and climate change by absorbing an enormous quantity of carbon dioxide from the atmosphere. In 1987, UNESCO declared the Sunderbans National Park a World Heritage Site.

The villagers in the Sunderbans live mostly on an island between the two forks of a wide river named Durga Duani, a section of the river Hooghly. The agrarian land, though fertile, is not enough to sustain all the villagers; many of them searching for alternate means of livelihood have to explore the mangrove forests across the river. Usually these people enter the forest in small groups and are guided by a leader known as a *beday*, or *baulay*, who not only understands the forest well, but is believed to possess some magical power to confuse the tigers. In the jungles they cut wood and the large fan-shaped Golpata leaves for fuel, or collect honey from the many beehives atop the trees. There are several "widows' villages" in the Sunderbans where most male members of the family have been killed by tigers. Such a village is easily recognised by a fluttering piece of white cloth tied conspicuously on

The bustling Gosaba Port in the Sunderbans

Figurines of Bon Bibi goddess and her brother Shah Jungli

a treetop near the house. Fatalistic as they are, the people believe that apart from the benevolent Bon Bibi they have no other saviour to rely upon. Bon Bibi is the powerful reigning deity in the Sunderbans who, with the help of her warrior brother Shah Jungli, protects her subjects—the woodcutters, honey collectors and fishermen—from the wrath of the dreaded Dakshinray, the Tiger Lord. People have great faith in the might and kindness of the goddess—in every village they have built a shrine for Bon Bibi. Various myths and legends are associated with the goddess who is greatly revered by both the Hindus and Muslims.

Gosaba, the nerve centre as well as the main entry point to the Sunderbans, is a small town and fishing port that serves Kolkata daily with large supplies of fresh fish. Here, one finds several people busy at work. Most conspicuous are the small girls combing the waters with hand nets, sifting the eggs of tiger prawns. Fully grown tiger prawns fetch a high price in Kolkata as well as the export market. But these young children standing all day in knee-deep water earn paltry wages, risking attacks by small sharks common in the rivers. At a village nearby, I had the opportunity of seeing for the first time a *dhenki*, a country-made device for husking paddy into

A young girl combing water with a net in search of tiger prawn seeds

rice. Although it is a fertile rice-producing zone, there is no rice mill in the Sunderbans for lack of electricity and importing costly diesel all the way from Kolkata is unaffordable.

Although I did not spot a live shark, while aboard a mechanised country boat (locally called *bhot-bhoti* for the characteristic sound it makes), I saw Gangetic dolphins as well as estuarine crocodiles and a gharial (fishing alligator) basking on the river banks—as soon as our vessel drew near they all slid into the water. Here, on the soft muddy soil along the river bank, I was shown fresh pug marks of a tiger that had possibly been there at dawn. At Sajnekhali, the forest headquarters, we noticed several sunbathing fiddler crabs with protruded eyes displaying their bright red bigger pincers—these extremely shy and

Left: Fiddler crabs on mud flats alongside a tiger's pug mark
Facing page: A village in the Sunderbans

tiny creatures would instantly disappear into their holes at the least movement. From our vessel we also saw a herd of chitals (spotted deer) on the other bank, feeding on the green leaves and shoots dropped by the monkeys in the trees. They also alert the deer if any tiger is spotted in the vicinity. *Bhot-bhotis* are the only means of local transport in this riverine area that ferries people, goods and cattle between the many islands scattered all over the Sunderbans.

Later that day it became windy and dark with threatening ominous clouds; incessant rains continued pouring through the afternoon, evening and night—a kind of downpour unimaginable in the dry upper inland zone. By the next day, a dense blanket of fog engulfed the surroundings making visibility impossible. The *bhot-bhoti* had been waiting to ferry me to Gosaba from where I would be able to reach Kolkata by road. While hurrying towards the jetty, I found myself entangled in ankle-deep slush and mud. All of a sudden I was yanked back by my companion; I was about to step on something which looked like a piece of rope. It was, in fact, a venomous krait that was struggling in the mud.

During its peak, the monsoon season can last for several months and villages in the Sunderbans lie submerged under knee-deep water and slush. This is also a time when snakes and other creatures come out of their inundated nesting holes. While trudging on the way a large boat caught our notice; it was stuck in the midst of many *shulos* (pointed spikes of sharp

Matla River in the Sunderbans

Numerous myths and legends associated with this mysterious pristine forest have influenced and enriched Bengal's history and literature. In the sixth century BC, a daring Bengali prince Vijay Simha and his 700 followers sailed across the Bay of Bengal and occupied the island of Lanka (Ceylon) establishing the kingdom of Simhal named after himself; he married a local princess and it is said their progeny are supposedly the ancestors of the present day people of Sri Lanka. Two famous Sri Lankan epics the Mahavansha and Deepavansha corroborate the story.

The famous ballad Manasa Vijaya written by the poet Bipradas (c. 1495) is based on the story of the valiant seafaring merchant Chand Saudagar, who used to sail with his fleet of cargo ships across the seas. Being a dedicated votary of Lord Shiva he would not accept Devi Manasa, the serpent-goddess as another deity to worship. Revengeful Manasa not only got his seven boats laden with riches drowned in the Bay of Bengal but also eliminated his six young sons through snake bite; Lakhinder, the well guarded last son too died similarly on his wedding night even though he was protected well inside a strong room built of steel. His devoted wife Behula had to pass through several agonising ordeals to appease the angry Manasa Devi, whereupon the goddess and the unrelenting Chand Saudagar came to terms and mutual reconciliation; all the sons of Chand regained their lives and their losses were fully restored. A small island called Neti Dhopani associated with the legend still exists in the inner Sunderbans as also do some ancient ruins reminiscent of Chand Saudagar.

The legendary 'Baro Bhuiyas' (twelve super landlords) who were independent rulers of south Bengal had defied the forces of the mighty Mughal emperors for years; decayed remnants of their coastal fortifications lie deserted in the Sunderbans till now.

A mangrove forest with aerial roots in the Sunderbans

Pilgrims at Ganga Sagar

aerial roots of the mangroves) covering the low sloping land beside our path; the boat had lost its way due to the combined effect of rains and high tide of the previous evening, and was stranded when the waters receded. To be afloat again it must wait till the next high tide comes which can be after several hours. Plenty of snails, tiny and big can be seen in this area, some of them measuring up to four inches in length.

During the Mughal regime, the Sunderbans had become the haven of Portuguese pirates called *harmad*s who would not only plunder, but also abduct people for the slave trade. The eastern part of the Sunderbans was also the target of frequent attacks from the Mags from the nearby state of Arakan adjacent to Burma (Myanmar), who were notorious for brutal savagery and cruelty. To the south of the Sunderbans lies the desolate island Sagardwip. Popularly called Ganga Sagar, this is a highly sacred place where during the Makar Sankranti festival held in mid-January every year, millions of devout pilgrims assemble to take dips at the holy confluence of the Ganga and pay homage to the river goddess as well as the great Puranic sage Maharshi Kapil who had his hermitage here.

A painting depicting Goddess Ganga riding the makara, a fish-monster

According to the Puranas, the celestial Ganga had descended on Earth acceding to the severe penance of the pious king Bhagiratha to wash away the sins and sanctify the mortal remains of Bhagiratha's ancestors accursed and annihilated by the angered sage Kapil. The place is the land's end in south Bengal; the mouth of the river Ganga is the widest here.

Over the past many centuries, this passage of the Ganga, also called the Hooghly River, has served as the main waterway for communication and trading between the northern plains of India and countries across the Bay of Bengal. But navigating ships through the mouth of the Hooghly is always fraught with great danger; at the bend of Diamond Harbour lies the submerged great sand bar obstructing the passage of large ships which are very likely to get stuck here, sometimes sunk or stranded forever. Ten kilometres further up is the dreaded and treacherous quicksand trap known as the James and Mary Danger Point, hidden under water where, in 1894, a British ship by this name sank.

The most dangerous zone starts from the confluence of the river Damodar, fifty kilometres south of Kolkata up to 'Hooghly Point' a few kilometres downstream, where the river Rupnarain has its confluence as well. These two tributaries, the Damodar and the Rupnarain continuously discharge huge deposits of silt into the Hooghly creating wide spread beds of soft alluvial clay and sand; the ever growing bulk of the amassed silt keeps shifting positions frequently. Any ship can sink within minutes as it happened in 1919 when *S.S. Sanctoria* sank off here—its top mast is still visible today. The Bengal Pilot Services have been alerting and helping all ships by providing a pilot boat that directs and guides the seafaring vessels safely to and from the confluence of the Hooghly with the sea and the port of Kolkata.

Fishing in the creeks of the Sunderbans

Hanseshwari Temple in Bansberia

In the past, ships coming from the Bay of Bengal could easily reach upstream of the Hooghly River for some fifty kilometres north of Kolkata without any hindrance. Saptagram (or Satgaon) the famous international port of Bengal in those days was located at the confluence of the Saraswati River, where the Portuguese traders had their post. Due to continuous silting, the mouth of the Saraswati was gradually choked, forcing the Portuguese to shift their base to Hooghly a few kilometres south. It was the same for the Dutch, French and Danish traders; all their ports gradually faded into oblivion as ships could not reach their posts due to the drying river bed. The southernmost port of Kolkata has somehow managed to survive resorting to regular dredging of the river bed; even then the navigability of the Hooghly is gradually dying down.

Coastal Bengal is known by its many foreign settlements that came up between the sixteenth and seventeenth century within eighty kilometres north of the river mouth; busy ports, factories and warehouses of European trading companies flourished on the banks of the Hooghly. Of these, the British trading post of Calcutta on the east bank established in 1698 surpassed all others in prosperity. To set up their fortified factory, the administrator Job Charnock of the British East India Company managed to acquire land from the village of Kalikata on lease from the Zamindar Saborno Chowdhury along with two adjacent villages, Sutanuti and Gobindapur. The lease was settled for a meagre amount of Rs. 1,300 annually, while the ruling Mughal Subehdar Azim-us-Shan (grandson of Emperor Aurangzeb) had to be paid Rs. 1,600! Kalikata as well as Saptagram or Satgaon find mention in Abul Fazal's *Ain-e-Akbari* (c. 1585) as well as in the epic *Chandimangal* written by the great Bengali poet Mukundaram. Charnock's Calcutta in the eighteenth century fast grew into prominence to become the capital of British India. In close proximity to Calcutta were also ports and

Bandel Church outside Kolkata

settlements of the other trading European powers; the trading Armenians were already in Calcutta while the Portuguese too had set up their factories in Bandel. The French had theirs at Chandernagar, the Danes were settled at Serampore and the Dutch at Chinsurah. With the passage of history all these ports have been decimated leaving behind small sleepy townships, some old and dilapidated buildings and several ancient temples and churches.

About forty kilometres north of Calcutta is the historic town of Hooghly that was once developed by the Portuguese as an important outpost, long before the rise of Job Charnock's Calcutta of the British East India Company; Satgaon (Bansberia) further upstream was their main and original centre, but due to silting of the river bed, both the ports had to be abandoned. In nearby Bandel, their other settlement, they built a church that was destroyed by Emperor Shah Jahan, only to be rebuilt. Chandernagar on the west bank was an important French post since 1673. Serampur, also in the vicinity was a progressive Danish centre where in 1799 two missionaries, Marshman and Carey established the first Indian printing press with the assistance of a local craftsman, Panchanan Karmakar, a skilled ironsmith. Carey also founded Serampur College. Close to Hooghly was the Dutch settlement of Chinsurah, where today, the church and cemetery are well preserved monuments.

A view of the Strand, Chandernagar

French Church in Chandernagar

Further north of Hooghly, on the west bank is Ambika Kalna (Kalna), once a vital ancient port known to the Romans, Arabs and the Chinese; the Greeks used to call it the City of Parthalis that connected north Indian cities on the waterways of the Ganga. Kalna was never a foreign settlement, but due to gradual silting of the river bed and with the introduction of the railways, the port lost its importance, dying a natural death; the old city now survives with its superb terracotta temples and the heritage of weaving fine textiles. For centuries Bengal's textiles—especially the "woven air" muslins—were coveted by the outside world; in the great Roman empire, at the celebrated Ming court in China as well as in the markets of Europe, Egypt, the Middle East and Southeast Asia, the wonderful gossamer-like muslin was in tremendous demand. Bengal's great tradition of weaving had been forcibly

The ancient river port, Kalna, on the Ganga River at Hooghly

An ornate pillar of the Lalji Temple at Ambika Kalna

Above: Kalighat artists
Facing page: Fourteenth century figure of Goddess Parvati at Tribeni ghat, Hooghly

Calcutta (now Kolkata) got its name from a small nondescript village Kalikata or Kalikshetra, the highly venerated and very ancient shrine of Goddess Kali. According to Puranic legend, the corpse of Parvati (Lord Shiva's consort) was dismembered into many pieces. One of her fingers landed here, sanctifying the place as a *peethasthana* (an important place of pilgrimage). Originally, the ancient terracotta temple of 1809 was built by the *zamindar* (land owner) of Barisha in the traditional *aatchala* style architecture of Bengal; the temple as seen today has come up after several major renovations since then. Revered as the place of Goddess Kali, an incarnate of Parvati or Shakti, the holy shrine of Kalighat attracts devotees from all parts of India. Kalighat is also known for its traditional art of *pata* (scroll) painting and painted *sara* (clay saucer) a popular form of folk art.

Left: A weaver from Kalna at the weekly Saree Haat
Below: Fine Indian muslin woven by Rabi Saha
passes through a ring

suffocated, almost destroyed during the rule of the East India Company for its commercial interest to create a free market of factory-made inferior British cloth in India. However, the muslin industry has now been revived once again.

In Kalna, Sri Rabi Saha, a President's award winning weaver, weaves a five metre length of weightless muslin which can easily pass through a ring on his finger!

The Dutch also had a fortified warehouse at Falta, forty kilometres downstream of Calcutta where the British had retreated when Nawab Siraj-ud-Daula captured Calcutta, the British stronghold in 1756. South of Falta the Rupnarain River joins the Hooghly close to the Bay of Bengal. Near their confluence lies the ancient historic city of Tamluk that was known to the old world as the flourishing Indian port-city of Tamralipta or Tamralipti. Tamralipta finds mention in various scriptures as well as in the epic *Mahabharata*. In the later period during the rule of the Mauryan Emperor Ashoka and others of his dynasty, it was a celebrated Buddhist centre of India for over a thousand years. According to the accounts of the Chinese travelling monk Huen-Tsang, the Buddha, while coming from Magadha had visited several parts of Kalinga (Odisha) and Vanga (Bengal) to propagate his message of peace and non-violence; Tamralipta was at the forefront of these places where Emperor Ashoka had erected stupas and monasteries to commemorate the Buddha's visit. Fa-Hien, the other renowned Chinese pilgrim also spent two years here studying Buddhism and visiting monasteries. However, after the Mauryan rule, a mystic form of Buddhism developed in Bengal during the monarchy of the Pala dynasty that changed the course and history of Buddhism. Tamralipta or Tamluk became a major part of this historical change converting Buddhism to a typical Tantric form of mysticism that ultimately had assimilated the Shakti cult of Bengal. The prominent Buddhist Tantric Goddess Tara (Devi Ugratara) became a manifestation of Goddess Kali (Shakti) being worshipped in Bengal as Devi Bargabhima, the reigning deity of Tamluk. The 1,200-year-old shrine of the Devi is regarded as an important *peethasthan* (or sacred place).

Tamluk is also known for its Vaishnavite cult. According to the epic *Mahabharata* edited by both Jaimini (a disciple of the great sage Veda Vyasa) and Kashiram Das, a celebrated Bengali poet, Arjuna the third Pandava came here accompanying Lord Krishna to set free the horse dedicated for the Ashwamedha Yagna to be performed by Maharaja Yudhisthira; the horse was arrested by the ruling king Tamradhwaja of Tamralipta who defied the sovereignty of Yudhisthira.

Tamluk was once a centre of Christianity too, when in the seventeenth century it became a Portuguese settlement. A Catholic church was built

A view from the Esplanade, Calcutta 1850

here in 1635. It became their centre for conversion of the local people to Christianity as well as for the slave trade. However, the Mughal forces under Emperor Shah Jahan had ultimately destroyed the Portuguese stronghold. Once again in 1942 Tamluk came to the limelight during the Quit India movement which Mahatma Gandhi led against the ruling British. Matangini Hazra, a spirited lady leading a crowd in this non-violent agitation fell to the bullet of the police in her attempt to free the administrative building from British control. Attributed by Mahatma Gandhi as a *Veerangana*, her memorial was raised here soon after the country won freedom. Tamluk is presently the headquarters of the Purba Medinipur District of West Bengal.

During the British rule, Bengal had been the most important and progressive realm of the British Empire. The nineteenth and twentieth centuries were the age of Renaissance for Bengal's social, cultural and political consciousness, including an upsurge in the field of religion and philosophy.

The country witnessed the emergence of several great personalities who enriched the history and heritage of India. Immortal among those Bengali celebrities are Raja Ram Mohan Roy, Ishwarchandra Vidyasagar, Bankim Chandra Chatterjee, Rabindranath Tagore, Michael Madhusudan Dutt, Sir J.C. Bose, Acharya P.C. Ray, Ramakrishna Paramahansa, Swami Vivekananda, Sri Aurobindo, Chittaranjan Das, Surendranath Banerjee, Subhas Chandra Bose and a host of others.

To these great names may be added the later celebrities like Satyajit Ray and Mother Teresa. Bengalis, Kolkatans in particular, are proud of Bengal's great cultural heritage, and of their bustling state capital that was the capital of British India till 1911. Called the 'City of Palaces' in the early days of the Raj, Kolkata in recent years has earned several derisive epithets too such as 'the city of processions', 'the city of pavement shops' or the 'city of eateries' and so on. However, in spite of its squalor and confusion it is the 'city of joy' for all Kolkatans—a city with a noble and spacious heart to welcome everyone in its friendly fold.

The prosperity of Calcutta was hindered when the capital of British India was shifted to Delhi in 1911. The rulers wanted to curb the growing spirit of Indian Nationalism of which Bengal or Calcutta was the rallying force. Unfortunately, calamities befell Bengal one after the other. First came the severe man-made famine of 1943, when hundreds and thousands of the villagers rushed to the city in search of food but perished of starvation on the streets. Then, prior to India's winning freedom from the British in 1947 came the great communal violence killing thousands. Thereafter, came the partition of Bengal, and the exodus of millions of people who fled from East Bengal (now Bangladesh) in search of shelter, security and a living. Before the city could sustain this abrupt influx of population came another bewildering surge of refugees from across the border when the Bangladesh Liberation War broke out in 1971.

Overburdened with the unprecedented population explosion, the state administration and economy went askew. This apart, even under normal conditions, crowds from various corners of India as well as from the neighbouring countries of Bangladesh and Nepal are also being drawn to this hospitable metropolis. For a large majority of these immigrants, pavements

Interior of an antique palatial mansion in North Kolkata

on the roadside are the home where they have set up semi-permanent dwellings and would fight tooth and nail to survive against all adversities.

Due to the partition of Bengal, Calcutta had lost its industrial hinterlands which were in East Bengal. This resulted in the closure of numerous factories and jute mills, the main source of state revenue. The other revenue earner, the port, is steadily losing importance due to heavy silting of the river Hooghly that prevents big ships from entering. These complex predicaments have resulted over time in severe economic constraints that have been long haunting the city. A major section of the city's less privileged citizens thrive as hawkers or small traders occupying street pavements for varied professions while the city as a whole looks like a sea of shops selling vegetables, varied knick-knacks. Hordes of eateries and tea stalls crowd the curbside.

Job Charnock's Calcutta was established around the first Fort William of the British located on the sides of the big tank Lal Dighi which the Englishmen referred to as the Tank Square. The small habitation comprising principally of the Writers' Building, the Old Court, St. James Church and a few other imperial buildings were then known as 'White Calcutta' that had later expanded further, mainly towards the east, developing as Chowringhee and Park Street zone. This was the stretch in the Gobindapur area where the Englishmen lived, while the 'Black' Calcutta of Sutanuti, in the north was the acclaimed habitation of traditional Bengali aristocrats and big established merchants known as the Seths and Basaks. In the South was the ancient place of Kalikshetra with its holy shrine of Goddess Kali and all that forming a small township of Kalikata. With the passage of time all three isolated habitations further expanded and merged to grow as the great metropolis of Calcutta, the grand capital of the British Empire in India now renamed Kolkata.

Several prominent and iconic landmarks adorn today's Kolkata. The Rabindra Setu (Howrah Bridge) built in 1941 over the Hooghly River connects Kolkata with the city of Howrah where the main railway terminus is located. It is the third highest cantilever bridge in the world with a single span of 1,480 feet that replaced the earlier pontoon bridge of 1874. During the peak of summer the all-steel bridge expands in length by another three feet. The busiest bridge in the world, its flow of traffic exceeds 65,000 vehicles a day and countless pedestrians. However, to reduce the continuing heavy pressure of vehicular traffic a second bridge, the Vidyasagar Setu has now been constructed over the Hooghly further south.

The Ochterlony Monument in the eastern part of the Maidan is another major landmark; this 158-foot-tall column was raised in honour of Sir David Ochterlony who won the Nepal Wars of 1814-1816. Located on the eastern part of the vast expanse of open field called the Maidan, this monument has become the traditional site for various political meetings and rallies. The structure is now re-named Shaheed Minar in memory of the great many freedom fighters who had laid down their lives to liberate the country from British rule.

In 1773 the present Fort William, named after King William I of England, was built on the east bank of the Hooghly River, replacing the earlier one in Job Charnock's Calcutta, which was located further north around the Lal Dighi. The extensively built present fort is a self-contained city by itself. For its all round development the ancient village of Gobindapur had to be

Howrah Bridge in Kolkata by night

evacuated and the forest in its vicinity had to be cleared to create the space for the new fort, leaving a vast expanse of open land on three sides, with the Ganga or Hooghly rivers on the west. This was necessary to facilitate free firing range for guns. Though no gun had ever been fired in battle, the vast clear ground around the fort till now remains and is called the Maidan, a great expanse of open plane land where no construction is permitted. This wide grassy open field serves as the 'lungs' of the crowded metro city of Kolkata; today, the Maidan is at the heart of the world of sports where various games like football and cricket are played all year round.

Early in the morning, the Maidan is frequented by morning walkers, and is a parade ground for the NCC cadets; by the afternoon it turns into a venue for all political meetings and rallies; on Sundays the Maidan becomes a carnival ground, filled with astrologers, jugglers and magicians, besides vendors selling spicy snacks. In the last few years, it has also been the venue of the most popular and celebrated annual Book Fair of Kolkata as well as

*Right: Parrots cooling off under a fountain at
Eden Garden in Kolkata
Below: The Maidan, Kolkata*

for various other fairs and exhibitions.
The historic Hindu (Swadeshi) Mela
held here in the late nineteenth century
played an important role in promoting
the spirit of Indian nationalism when the
poet Rabindranath Tagore, then a boy of
fifteen, made his first public appearance
in the Mela. The famous Ranji Cricket
Stadium is on the northern end of the
Maidan. Next to it is the Netaji Indoor
Stadium, the largest of its kind in Asia.
Eden Garden, the charming park nearby is named after Ashley Eden,
the Governor of Bengal (1877–82). In the vicinity are several imposing
buildings raised during the period of the Raj—the High Court, a 180-foot-

tall structure in the Gothic style is a replica of
the famous Staadhause of Ypres, Belgium; its
central tower is actually taller than the soaring
Ochterlony Monument or the Shaheed Minar by
15 feet. Nearby stands the Town Hall in Doric
architecture; in its front is the Assembly House.

The Raj Bhavan (Government House) is also
close by; to its west is the St. John's Church built
in 1787. Abounding in tombstones, the church
precincts have many interesting graveyards of
historic personalities—the grave of Job Charnock,
the founder of British Calcutta who died in 1787 is
housed inside an octagonal mausoleum. Admiral
Watson, the colleague of Lord Clive has also been
laid to rest here. Further north is the BBD Bagh
named after three young revolutionaries, Benoy,

Badal and Dinesh, who were executed by the British rulers. The area around Lal Dighi demarcated Job Charnock's Calcutta in the beginning; it was later named Dalhousie Square after the name of Lord Dalhousie, the Governor General, and finally became BBD Bagh, the Heritage Site of Kolkata after India won freedom. Across the Lal Dighi is the red sprawling Writers' Building that was earlier the office site of the writer clerks of the East India Company; presently it houses the administrative machinery of the West Bengal government; in the west stands the imposing building of the General Post Office built in Corinthian architecture; in the east is the St. Andrews

Kirk that was built on the site of a court (Old Court) where Maharaja Nanda Kumar had been tried.

At the southern end of the Maidan stands the immaculate palatial building, the sprawling Victoria Memorial with its dazzling great dome and the flying fairy on top—an Italian bronze figure serves as the weathercock. This charming memorial with its all-white marble edifice outshines all the other landmarks of the metropolis with its sheer beauty and grandeur. Built by the renowned Martin Company of Calcutta its architecture follows the Italian Renaissance style. Like the Taj Mahal in Agra, all its marbles came from the mines of Makrana in Rajasthan.

In commemoration of Queen Victoria, it was after her death that the Memorial was conceived of by Lord Curzon, the Viceroy. The foundation stone was laid in 1906 by George V, the grandson of the Queen, the then Prince of Wales. Upon completion in 1921 it was inaugurated by the Queen's great grandson, Edward VIII, also the Prince of Wales. The cost of ten crore rupees was met by the rulers of princely states of India and some distinguished Indian nobility. This lavishly built memorial is a veritable museum of various relics of the long British rule in India, preserving some 3,500 memorabilia of the Queen and the British Raj. An expanse of charming park with greenery surrounds the memorial building while a vast sheet of water reflects all its architectural grandeur. At the centre of the frontal garden facing the main entrance is the majestic bronze figure of the Queen in all her regalia. Outside her grand marble pedestal, facing east is an excellent

Heritage buildings on the Esplanade, Kolkata

bronze sculpture depicting an Indian panorama of a festive procession. Several marble statues of imperial celebrities decorate the garden. In the evening the memorial building is well illuminatcd when sound and light shows are held reviving the glorious history of the Raj.

The Memorial has a unique treasure of superb paintings made by foreign artists depicting various Indian scenes, and of ancient Calcutta in particular. The paintings by the two Daniels, Thomas and William, and those of Emily Eden, sister of Viceroy Lord Auckland are part of this precious collection. The largest of them all is an oil painting, titled *Arrival of HRH Albert Edward, Prince of Wales, at Jaipur.* Apart from various valuable manuscripts, the notebooks of Tipu Sultan, Abul Fazal's *Ain-e-Akbari* and the *Akbarnama* by Allami are also there. The Queen's Hall in the centre houses the standing marble figure of the Queen in her youth; the ceiling above is adorned with twelve charming frescoes. The Durbar Hall gallery displays many historical exhibits—a letter written by Maharaja Nandakumar, the swords of Haider Ali and Tipu Sultan, and a snuff-box of

Victoria Memorial lit up in the evening

Bronze sculpture of the royal procession heralding the Delhi Durbar, Victoria Memorial Hall

Warren Hastings among other exhibits. The Calcutta Gallery highlights the history of British India's capital as it was till 1911.

East of Victoria Memorial stands the elegant St. Paul's Cathedral, an important church of India consecrated in 1847 by Bishop Wilson. It is a sprawling white building, the first Episcopal Church of the East. The cathedral is beautifully decorated with stained glass windows. The cultural hub of present day Kolkata is located around this part of the Maidan. The Academy of Fine Arts is a permanent meeting ground for artists and is a cultural centre as well. The adjacent institutions, Rabindra Sadan as well as the Bangla Academy are celebrated venues of dance, drama and music. Nandan, another cultural institution houses the famous Satyajit Ray Archives. On Sarat Bose Road in the Bhowanipore area, is the ancestral residence of India's great patriot, Netaji Subhash Chandra Bose, which is now a museum.

College Street in central Kolkata, popularly known as Boi Para is notable for its widespread zone of book shops and publishing houses. Numerous shops, flanking the wide road, sell all kinds of books. From the pavement shops of College Street, overflowing with old books, on some occasions, one can even discover rare antique publications for a pittance.

The celebrated Albert Hall is like an island, its famous India Coffee House is the traditional rendezvous of the intellectuals of Kolkata where I once spotted the maestro Satyajit Ray enjoying a cup of coffee over a heated discussion. Albert Hall happened to be the venue of the first National Conference held by the Indian National Congress in 1885. The other notable place in the ancient Sutanuti area is the old Tagore House at Jora Sanko bearing a vivid cultural ambience of its own. In an old eighteenth century house, now named Rabindra Mancha, the great poet Rabindranath Tagore was born on 7 May 1861. He died here on 7 August 1941 and both days are reverently observed in his memory throughout Bengal. The Tagore Museum and the Rabindra Bharati University are located here.

An important zone in north Kolkata, between the famous Chitpore Road—the oldest street in the city, and the Ganges River is the interesting area of Kumartuli, Kolkata's celebrated potter's quarters. In this area a few hundred ateliers live in a dense, beehive-like concentration where these talented artisans have worked for generations making sublime images of various gods—Durga, Lakshmi, Saraswati and Kali, the elephant-headed Ganesha and many others. These gifted potters now settled in Kolkata hail from the internationally famous doll making centre of Krishnanagar, 200 kilometres north-east of Kolkata. It is interesting to watch their ways of crafting immaculate figures of gods out of simple clay. Even small children are able to mould charming, delicate clay figurines with their nimble fingers.

In autumn, Durga Puja the biggest festival for Bengalis is celebrated all over Bengal with great pomp and splendour; most of the exquisite images of the gods are made at Kumartuli.

The adjoining localities of Shovabazar, Chitpore, Bagbazar and Shyambazar in north Kolkata are constituent areas of village Sutanuti of the ancient days. It is the place where traditional Bengali homes, many of them being palatial buildings in reality, can be seen or even visited. The people

Clay idols being made (above) and painted (below) in Kumartuli, north Kolkata

living in this area are friendly and are pleased to show people around their ancestral homes.

The eastern border of the Maidan that was earlier the ancient settlement of Gobindapur, is bounded on the east by the areas of Esplanade, Chowringhee and Park Street, a zone of high rise palaces and mansions raised in the days of the British Raj, of which the Indian Museum is most important. It is not

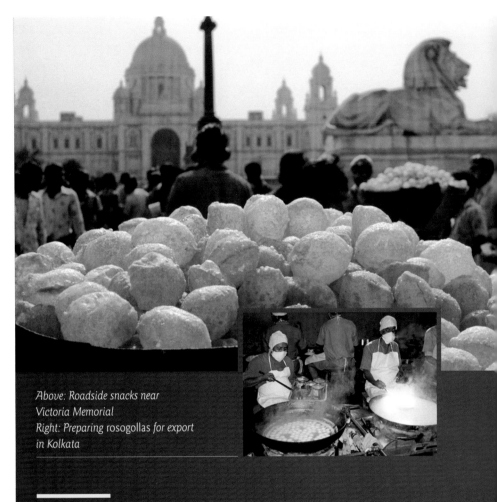

Above: Roadside snacks near Victoria Memorial
Right: Preparing rosogollas for export in Kolkata

North Kolkata is reputed for its traditional expertise in preparing various kinds of delectable Bengali sweets. The recipes for these sweets are part of the centuries-old heritage passed on through generations, which has now spread all over the city. The *rosogolla*, it is said, is the great invention of one Nabin Chandra Das of Bagbazar about 200 years ago; now his aspiring successors have expanded the ancestral business setting up a modern plant from where sweets in vacuum sealed cans are being exported abroad. Legends also glorify another tasty delicacy, the Ladycani; it is said that this unique sweet was a special inventive preparation made for Lady Canning, wife of the ruling Governor General.

Devotees worshipping Goddess Durga during Durga Puja

merely the largest in India but is also considered one of the best in Asia for its repository of rare treasures of Buddhist Gandharan art. The National Library in Alipore, south-west Kolkata is another important landmark. Named Belvedere House, it was the residence of the former Lieutenant Governor of Bengal in the nineteenth century. The largest library of India preserves nearly 1.7 million books in addition to half-a-million archival documents attracting over a thousand readers daily. Located in the vicinity are the famed Zoological Park as well as the vast Agri-horticultural Society Garden. The Kolkata zoo boasts of its oldest and unique member—a 260-year-old giant turtle named 'Adwaita' belonging to the rare species of Giant Tortoise, originally inhabiting the waters of the Indian Ocean around the islands of Seychelles.

Kolkata is also known for its 225-year-old Botanical Garden which is located across the Ganga at Sibpur in the district of Howrah. Founded by Colonel Kyd in 1786 as a retreat, it is the oldest botanical garden of India, now spread over 272 acres of land containing endless species of trees and exotic plants. The chief attraction is the enormous 350-year-old banyan tree, the world's largest.

A rather venerated place in Kolkata is the Missionaries of Charity located near Entally Market in the city centre. It was founded by the Nobel Laureate Mother Teresa who dedicated her life to serving the poor and the downtrodden.

Other than at Kalighat, the religious pursuit of the Bengalis can also be seen in the suburbs of Dakshineshwar and Belur in the north of Kolkata. A weekly visit to either of these places, Dakshineshwar in particular is a must for many Kolkatans. Dakshineshwar is known for its association with Sri Ramakrishna Paramahansa, the great philosopher and priest of the goddess, who was the religious Guru (preceptor) of Swami Vivekananda. Visits to Dakshineshwar are best on a Sunday morning as it is the most opportune day and time to enjoy the ambience of the exquisite shrine of Devi Bhabotarini (Goddess Kali) built by Rani Rashmoni in 1847. The approach to the temple is shaded under big trees, where groups of monkeys often approach visitors to check their bags, and even their pockets for treats. Within the temple precinct a serpentine queue of devotees often reaches up to the temple door.

Many of them come to pay obeisance to Ma Bhabotarini and her consort Lord Shiva in the twelve temples on the riverside promenade; they also visit the room of Thakur Ramakrishna, Ma Sarada and the sacred Panchabati, his place of meditation on the secluded banks of the Ganges River. The river ghat is crowded with people taking a holy dip. Boatmen solicit passengers for a trip to Belur on the opposite bank across, advertising their services at the top of their voices.

Kali Temple, Dakshineshwar

The ornate façade of an old mansion in north Kolkata

Belur Math is a spectacular grand complex of Ramakrishna Temple and other buildings. The principal structure is an ingenious synthesis of several architectural styles representing a Hindu temple, an Islamic mosque and the Christian church. The temple, built in 1938, preserves the mortal remains of Sri Ramakrishna Paramahansa enshrined here by his great disciple, Swami Vivekananda in 1898. The complex is the headquarters of the worldwide Ramakrishna Mission, also founded by him.

Sunrise at Puri

Odisha

The eastern coastline of Bengal after the sea resort of Digha enters Chandaneshwar in the state of Odisha that was once known as the kingdom of Kalinga. From here the hinterland, between the sea shore dotted with fishing villages and the hills of the Eastern Ghat, presents a view of a predominantly vast green fertile agrarian plane. The people, many of them from the tribal region, possess an ancient seafaring heritage. Cargo ships from Odisha laden with varied Indian goods once used to sail across the seas to many foreign countries. Such ships have been depicted in stone sculptures decorating the façade of the Puri Temple as well as the Brahmeshwar shrine of the capital Bhubaneshwar. The state economy largely depends on agriculture which unfortunately suffers too often due to frequent droughts as well as by the annual flooding of the rivers and violent cyclones in the coastal area during the monsoon season. Odisha, though rich in

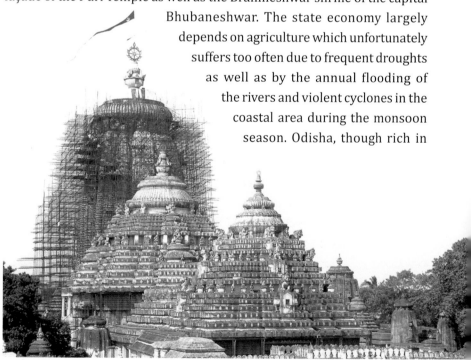

The domes of the Jagannath Temple in Puri

A tussor wall hanging of a patachitra painting

minerals, with large iron ore deposits in particular, is yet to utilise its wealth fully and effectively. But the talented artisans and craftsmen of the land are world famous for their various creative skills, be it immaculate stone carving, *patachitra* (scroll) painting, weaving exquisite textiles, crafting delicate silver filigree artifacts or even the graceful classical dance form of Odissi.

The beach at Chandipur is a recently developed and popular sea resort like West Bengal's Digha nearby. The interesting feature of the beach is that during low tide, the water recedes nearly five kilometres into the sloping seabed allowing light vehicles to ply on the sand. In recent years, the Indian Space Research Organisation (ISRO) has established its missile launching centre at Chandipur. Baleshwar in the north was earlier an old business centre for the Dutch, French, Danish and British traders who had set up their factories during the seventeenth-eighteenth century. The name of Baleshwar once again came to the limelight in 1915, when several young Bengali revolutionaries led by Bagha Jatin seeking independence from colonisation, gave up their lives in a bloody encounter with British police on the banks of Buri Balam River.

The old city of Cuttack, in the southwest, on the bank of Mahanadi River was the state capital earlier; presently Cuttack is an important trading centre; the city boasts of its Ravenshaw Collegiate School where Netaji Subhash Chandra Bose was once a student. His ancestral home is still preserved as a national museum. From the river ghat near the decimated Barabati Fort, local people annually celebrate Odisha's ancient seafaring tradition of Bali Yatra (voyage to the island of Bali for trading in Southeast Asia) on Purnima (full moon) night in the month of Kartik (November); small decorated replica boats on water are floated in commemoration of the glorious events of the past. Paradip on the sea coast not too far away is presently the only port of Odisha.

The monotony of the coastal scene is broken by the greenery of the Bhitarkanika wildlife sanctuary spread over the estuary of the river Brahmani. This marine sanctuary has the largest mangrove ecosystem in India after the Sunderbans; out of the seventy-two species of mangroves identified in the world, this one sanctuary alone is the home of sixty-three varieties. It is also a noted breeding ground for estuarine crocodiles, some of them growing to more than twenty feet in length! The Gahirmatha Sanctuary nearby happens to be one of the three mass breeding sites in the world of

the endangered green Olive Ridley turtles, who annually come here from the Pacific Islands to lay their eggs.

The kingdom of Kalinga was conquered by the Mauryan Emperor Ashoka in 260 BC. In the fierce battle that took place, over a hundred thousand people were killed with almost an equal number of the injured being taken captive. Bitterly anguished and repentant at the meaningless bloodshed and suffering of the innocent, Ashoka was determined to banish war and violence; he embraced Buddhism and spread the message of peace and non-violence far and wide in his vast empire. The Kesaris dynasty replaced the Mauryans in the second century AD and ruled Odisha for nearly 1,000 years; Hinduism was restored during this period and great temples were built in honour of Lord Jagannath at Puri, Tribhubaneshwar (Lingaraj) at Bhubaneshwar and later the colossal Sun Temple at Konark. Quite justifiably, Odisha may be called the land of

A swamp deer at the Bhitarkanika Sanctuary

Pilgrims at the Lingaraj Temple, dedicated to Lord Shiva

temples as would be evident on visiting these three cities mentioned.

Odishan culture and civilisation are the outcome of the traditional Bhakti cult woven on the religious strand of both Vaishnavism as well as Shaivism which later assimilated the spirit of Buddhism as well, after the Buddha was avowedly accepted as an 'avatar' (incarnate). However, the main spiritual fervour emanates from the reigning deity Lord Jagannath, an incarnation of Vishnu who resides at Shri Kshetra, Puri—the religious as well as the cultural hub of the state. Mahaprabhu Jagannath dominates the way of life in Odisha, the hereditary 'king' of Odisha functions by tradition as His empowered vassal. For the devout Indian pilgrims Jagannath Puri is one of the four holiest *dhams* (venerated shrine) in the country. The divine Jagannath aura culminates in the Rath Yatra festival celebrated in June-July when millions of people from all corners of the country assemble at Puri to witness the great ceremonial pulling of the massive, colourful and highly ornate wooden chariot of the Lord along with those of his brother

Balaram and sister Subhadra.

The annual Rath Yatra of Lord Jagannath is the most celebrated event of Odisha. This unique and colourful festival is held in commemoration of Lord Krishna's journey from Gokul to Mathura in the Puranic times. His wooden image (black-faced) along with those of his brother Balaram (white-faced), and sister Subhadra (yellow-faced) are taken out of the temple and placed on three different *raths* (carriages); the main carriage of Sri Jagannath is forty-five-feet-high, with a base of thirty-two-feet-square; the other cars are little smaller in size, each one mounted on sixteen large wheels measuring over six feet in diameter. The three stupendous carriages are dragged along on the wide Grand Road by numerous pullers engaged by the temple authority, besides the many pious pilgrims who consider pulling God's chariot to be a great virtue. Manoeuvering the colossal 'Juggernaut' is indeed a most complicated task as is the process of its halting. In the old days, fervent devotees used to sacrifice their lives under the wheels of the moving chariot in the belief that by doing so they would attain nirvana. The colourful journey ends at Gundicha Bari two kilometres away; here the gods 'rest' for seven days at their aunt's place before returning to the

Vaishnavites from abroad attending the Rath Yatra festival at Puri

Lord Jagannath, being a secular god is a great favourite of one and all, irrespective of caste and creed. For generations the tribal people have also been his devotees. The Puranic myth about Shri Kshetra or the sacred shrine states that the holy temple was built by King Indradyumna of the Surya dynasty. While asleep, the king received divine instructions to make use of the log of wood that would come from the sea floating ashore, in carving out the figure of Jagannath. Actually, the log contained the heart of Sri Krishna who sacrificed himself to the sea; thereby only his mortal body was destroyed but not the heart that came back floating in the form of a log. By the king's order an artisan—the celestial engineer Vishwakarma in disguise—took up the task of carving out the holy figure on the condition that he would be working in isolation, totally undisturbed till the images were complete. However, after several days of waiting when out of impatience the anxious queen opened the door of the closed chamber, the divine sculptor vanished in the air leaving behind the unfinished crude images of the deities which then had to be installed in a temple.

Idol of Lord Jagannath

Rath Yatra or 'Chalanti Pratima' in procession to Gundicha Bari

Devotees at the Rath Yatra

Shri Kshetra temple thereafter

Every year, the carriages are constructed anew; the old ones are dismantled and sold as sacred souvenirs or used as firewood in the large community kitchen of the temple. The wooden images of the gods are rebuilt every fifteen to twenty years when the priests and astrologers decide the auspicious hours depending upon the alignment of the stars and planets suitable for the rites.

The shrine as seen now was built in AD 1198 by King Anangabhima Deva in place of the original and ancient one. However, the images enshrined in the temple retain their original unfinished features. Puri has been identified as the ancient port-city of Dantpur, from where it is believed, that the hidden sacred tooth of the Buddha had been sent away to Kandy in Sri Lanka during the later Maurya period. The annual Kandy festival procession of the Buddha bears great similarity with the Puri Rath Yatra.

After the Jagannath temple, the other great attraction in Puri is the sea. The beach at Puri offers a stunning view of the Bay of Bengal and its sprawling lively shore. One can spend hours at the beach, watching the rolling silver surf that breaks on the shore. The receding water leaves behind a myriad of tiny sea shells of various shapes and colours; beachcombing visitors often collect these exotic shells. *Nulias* (fishermen) wearing conical caps take visitors on a ride across the waves on their primitive catamarans, a highly thrilling experience for the adventurous. However, much more enjoyable though less adventurous, would be taking a plunge in the surging waves being assisted by a *nulia* who all are expert swimmers. A solitary walk along the beach in the still dark hours of dawn can be quite rewarding.

Before sunrise, the eastern horizon becomes ruddy and dramatic. The spectacular fiery disc of the sun emerges, almost as if straight out of the sea, turning the water into molten gold. The fishing boats return at around this time with their freshly hauled catch. The men become busy emptying their nets and sorting out fish in separate heaps. On particular mornings, a formation of pious devotees proceed towards Gambhira singing devotional songs all the way with the accompaniment of tinkering cymbals. Gambhira is the sacred place where Sri Chaitanya Dev, a great Vaishnavite saint of Bengal had spent eighteen long years in meditation and worship of Lord Jagannath.

Built over a large area of 640-feet-square, the sprawling Shri Kshetra temple complex is surrounded by a high wall. A second wall inside encloses the sanctum proper. In the interior there are many closets, corridors and large halls, mostly dark and congested at many places. The temple precinct

Fishermen hauling in the day's catch, Puri

A village school near Puri

has four different entries. The Lion Gate guarded by two large figures of lions on the wide Grand Road is the main entrance. Others are the Elephant Gate, the Tiger Gate and one more under the protection of two horse riders. Temple architecture follows the conventional Odishan style—the *deul* (sanctum), *naat mandir* (dancing hall), *bhog mandap* (dining hall) and *jagmohan* (hall of audience). The *deul* being the highest at 192 feet enshrines the wooden images of the three deities, Balaram, Jagannath and Subhadra in the company of some lesser deities. On top of the conical temple tower is the *sudarshan chakra* (disc-like weapon) of Lord Vishnu together with his large fluttering flag, all visible from the distant sea. In the old days, seafaring sailors used to identify Puri from a distance recognising the soaring white temple and pinnacle called the White Pagoda as a landmark as against the Black Pagoda of Konark. Jagannath is open to all Hindus, irrespective of caste or creed. Currently, only Hindus are allowed into this ancient temple.

Located near Puri, the picturesque village Raghurajpur at first glance looks like any other nondescript serene rural habitation of Odisha. Set amidst tall coconut groves on the banks of a meandering brook, the village is one of the great centres of Odisha's varied traditional art forms. Everyone living in Raghurajpur is an artist in some way or the other, be it the art of

A village scene at Raghurajpur

Left: Patachitra *painter, Jagabandhu Mahapatra; Right: An etched palm leaf*

drawing *patachitras* (scroll paintings) or the classical dance style of Odisha known as Odissi. Walking along the coconut-palm fringed village path, one comes across several seemingly humble thatched-roof homes each one of which is a veritable art gallery or studio of the gifted *patachitra* painters. Sri Jagabandhu Mahapatra is one such rare talented artist. A President's Award winner, he warmly received us inside his home and showed a large number of his exquisite artistry—an array of greatly accomplished paintings on dried *tal* (palm tree) leaves as well as on *tussor* (silk). Squatting on the earthen floor were his two young disciples busy with brush in hand amidst a circle formed by large sea shells used as palettes. The subjects of the paintings are mostly related to popular and religious themes, scenes from Hindu mythology, Lord Jagannath with brother Balaram and sister Subhadra, or even scenes from daily life in villages. Raghurajpur is also the home of the great maestro of Odissi dancer, Guru Kelu Charan Mahapatra who, prior to his initiation to the world of dance, was a *patachitra* painter.

Bhubaneshwar, the state capital, is veritably a city of temples abounding with a thousand shrines, many of which are now in ruins having been demolished during the Mughal invasion of the sixteenth century. The most imposing shrine of all is the majestic Lingaraj temple, a glowing tribute to Odishan temple architecture. The residing deity is Tribhubaneshwar (Lord of the Three Worlds) from whom the city got its name. The massive temple façade is ornately carved with intricate sculptures of nymphs, celestial figures and amorous couples. Other exquisite temples of Bhubaneshwar are the Rajarani, Mukteshwar and Parashurameshwar, all profusely decorated with fine sculptures. Further south, on the way to Puri is the small village of Pipli, known for its unique local industry of exquisite appliqué artifacts. In the seventeenth century, Pipli was an early Dutch settlement in the vicinity of the sea.

Rajarani Temple at Bhubaneshwar

Colourful appliqué work of Pipli

North-east of Puri on the sea shore is Konark, which is near the confluence of the Chandrabhaga River with the Bay of Bengal, once a flourishing port. Konark is famous for its magnificent temple dedicated to the Sun God. The colossal temple shaped like a great chariot made of black weathered sandstone once stood as a landmark on the beach and was visible from a great distance to the navigating sailors on the sea. The sea has since receded a few kilometres away from the shrine. Konark Sun Temple is a thirteenth century monument built by Kalinga King Narasimhadeva I of the Ganga Dynasty in celebration of his victory over the Muslims.

Later, in the seventeenth century it fell to the Mughal army when the temple was ransacked, desecrated and deserted. For a long period since then it remained in ruins, covered with shrubs. The Archaeological Survey of India (ASI) salvaged the dilapidated temple in 1904 clearing the sand and debris and restoring it to its present look. The temple is a World Heritage Site as was declared by the UNESCO in 1984, and happens to be one of the Seven Wonders of India. It is dedicated to Surya (Arka), the Sun God and the huge structure is densely decorated with the finest carvings.

The entire temple complex is designed in the form of a colossal chariot drawn by seven spirited horses on twelve pairs of exquisitely ornamental gigantic wheels. The entrance to the temple is guarded by two giant lions sculpted in stone, each of which is crushing under its paws a war elephant, which in turn tramples a human figure. The temple symbolises the great majestic stride of the Sun God speeding along his celestial path. Three superb figures of Surya in green chlorite stone adorn the three sides of the temple in such orientation that they are each in turn illuminated by the rays of the sun in the morning, at noon and sunset.

The majestic edifice, though partly in ruins, still overwhelms the viewer with great wonder and regard for the highly skilled Odishan architects and sculptors of the bygone days. Seeing this amazing monumental synthesis of art and architecture, the poet Rabindranath Tagore paid his tribute with the words: "Here the language of stone surpasses the language of man". So impressed was he that he named one of his residences in Shantiniketan 'Konark'.

The imposing Konark Sun Temple

According to the Puranas, Samba the son of Krishna was cursed by his father and had to suffer from leprosy to repay a karmic debt. He had taken asylum at a secluded place then known as Maitreyaranya (later named Sambapuri) on the bank of river Chandrabhaga. Here he spent twelve years praying to the Sun God; finally, with his blessings he was cured. In commemoration of this mythological event people celebrate here holding a big annual fair in the month of Magha (January-February).

Sculpture of Surya, the Sun God at the Konark Sun Temple

The main sanctum of the gigantic temple was constructed 229-feet-high along with the audience hall 128 feet in height with elaborate external projections of large sculpted figures. The sanctum that enshrined the idol of Surya had fallen off in 1869; all that remain defying the vagaries of time and weather are the audience hall, the dancing hall and the dining hall. These massive and highly ornamental structures provide enough evidence that even in its present dilapidated state the Sun Temple till now is considered the foremost sublime monument of India, famous as much for its imposing dimensions and faultless proportions as for the harmonious interaction of its architectural grandeur in stone. The subject matter of the myriad carved depictions are varied images of deities, nymphs and human figures, birds and animals, musicians, dancers, lovers, scenes of courtly life, hunting and battle as well as charming floral and geometric designs. While going around the large complex one will find many erotic sculptures. After viewing these intently it becomes quite apparent that the frankness of their sensuous contents are truly the work of art, combining tender beauty with lyrical movements. They depict in all fullness the carnival of life with an overwhelming sense of appealing realism.

Intricately carved façade of the Sun Temple

Presently the temple precincts are the venue of Odisha's famous annual dance festival held in December. It may be worthwhile to mention that on 16 February 1980, Konark lay directly under the trajectory of the total solar eclipse, a rare event for the Sun Temple. On this great occasion a large number of photographers had assembled to record the unique celestial drama staged by the Sun over its own grand edifice on earth.

Further down the coast comes Lake Chilka, a large saltwater lagoon which is detached from the Bay of Bengal by a strip of sand bar and hillocks. Many small islands dotting the lake attract various migratory birds that flock here in large numbers during the winter. Birders can spot such feathered beauties like the flamingo, teal, bar-headed goose, pelican, white-bellied sea eagle and many others. Some of the birds migrate to India from faraway countries like Iran and Siberia, and there are the domestic shore birds too. Spread over an area of 1,100 square kilometres, the pear-shaped lake is fed by the rivers Daya and Bhargavi. Several islands with romantic names

Winter birds on Chilka Lake

Fisherwomen at Gopalpur

such as Breakfast Island and Honeymoon Island lie scattered in the lake. One can explore them by boats arranged at the tourist centres of Rambha, Balugaon and Satpada. During Makar Sankranti (celebrated in mid-January), the festival of Makar Mela is observed on the island of Kalijai. Cruising over the tranquil waters of the lagoon exploring some of these scenic islands is a unique experience.

Gopalpur-on-Sea, south of Lake Chilka, in the district of Ganjam bordering the state of Andhra Pradesh is a clean and peaceful beach resort devoid of crowds and squalor. During the days of the Raj it used to be a favourite holiday resort of the English, some of whom had settled here. In the seventeenth century Gopalpur happened to be an important Dutch port and fortified settlement. An ancient temple, an imposing lighthouse and a big fishermen's village are all that may be seen now.

*A view of
the Eastern Ghats*

Andhra Pradesh

The coastline, upon entering Andhra Pradesh, presents scenic views of charming golden beaches, one after the other, and lush green plains with the backdrop of low, russet hills. Mainly yielding paddy, this vast expanse of fertile land from the mouth of the Godavari River up to the delta of the Krishna River, is the rice bowl of the state. Unfortunately, these coves and the deltas on the coastline are annually devastated by the ravages of floods, cyclone and tidal waves causing immense loss of crops, property and life.

The 965-kilometre-long stretch of the Andhra coast begins from Ganjam and ends at Lake Pulicat on the border of Tamil Nadu. This portion of the eastern shoreline was once part of the legendary Coromandel Coast, during the reign of the powerful Chola Kings of the South; their vast empire extended far inside the northern states including Andhra Pradesh. There were several ports on this stretch of the east coast in those days having commercial linkage with Sri Lanka, Burma, Thailand, Malaya, Indonesia,

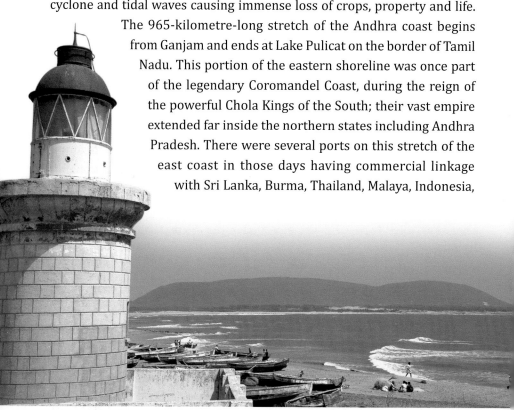

The old lighthouse and fishing harbour of Bheemunipatnam

Fish being dried on the way to Bheemunipatnam

Cambodia and others. With the expansion of trade, Indian culture, tradition and civilisation spread to those countries and even some Hindu kingdoms were established in Southeast Asia; Angkor Wat in Cambodia and Borobudur in Indonesia are world famous for their repositories of ancient Indian civilisation and architectural art heritage outside India. Another big Hindu kingdom called Majapahit also emerged in the thirteen century in eastern Java uniting parts of the Malay Peninsula.

Picturesque Bheemunipatnam, twenty-five kilometres north-east of Waltair or the modern port-city of Visakhapatnam, was an important Dutch port in the seventeenth century. Popularly called Bhimili, the port, though now abandoned, has a four-kilometre expanse of fine sea beach, an old but imposing lighthouse and some cottages inhabited by fishermen. The place has acquired its name from Bhima, one of the five Pandava brothers from the epic *Mahabharata*. According to legend, he had raised a temple here dedicating it to Lord Narasimha, the incarnate of Vishnu, which stands on a small hillock nearby. Bheemunipatnam is the oldest Dutch settlement on the Coromandel Coast. Ruins of the ancient Dutch fort and the old cemetery Hollanders Green are the notable memorabilia that now remain.

Vizag, the abbreviated British name for Visakhapatnam, was earlier a nondescript fishing harbour adjacent to the sea resort of Waltair. With the decline of Bheemunipatnam in the eighteenth century, the twin cities of Waltair and Vizag flourished as an excellent port with an ideal harbour, prospering as the second largest in the eastern coast after Chennai. Despite its steel plant, oil refinery, fertiliser factory, shipyard and naval base, Visakhapatnam is a quiet and pleasant modern city. Popularly called the 'Jewel of the East Coast' Visakhapatnam happens to be the second largest city of Andhra Pradesh and is also the headquarters of the Eastern Naval Command of India. The city won the National Tourism Award in 2009 for its excellent civic management and green practices.

A promontory of the Eastern Ghats jutting out of the sea protects the harbour and city from cyclones. Called the 'Dolphin's Nose' the long rocky projection looks quite similar in appearance to the figure of a floating dolphin. Of the two fine beaches that the city has, one is the three-kilometre-long Mission Beach that winds along the modern city and the wide Beach Road, terminating at the Ramakrishna Mission and Kali Bari Temple. The

Dutch cemetery at Bheemili Beach

A weekly market in the tribal area of the Eastern Ghats

other one, the six-kilometre-long Lawson's Beach, also known as Rishikonda, skirts the Waltair zone. A journey along the twenty-five-kilometre-long coastal route, an excellent all-weather highway leading from Visakhapatnam to the forgotten port Bheemunipatnam is a most enjoyable treat. Negotiating

Roadside shrine in Visakhapatnam

A view of the beach road at Visakhapatnam

numerous bends and curves of the shoreline fringing the brilliant expanse of the azure wavy sea, the wide open road passes through overhanging coconut palm and casuarina vistas with low, brown hills in the backdrop. Along the way are several fishing villages where colourfully dressed women

can be seen busy at work, neatly arranging heaps of freshly hauled fish to be dried under the sun.

Visakhapatnam, earlier known as Kulottungapattinam, got its present name from the warrior god Vaishakheshwara or Lord Kartikeya whose temple was built here in the eleventh century by the Andhra king proceeding to invade the kingdom of Varanasi; the temple is no more, having been washed away in a disastrous tidal wave about a hundred years ago. During the rule of Emperor Ashoka, Buddhism had spread extensively in the state. The ruins of several Buddhist sites have been unearthed in the coastal region. Amidst the low hills of the Eastern Ghats at Simhachalam, nineteen kilometres north of the city, stands an exquisite temple dedicated to Lord Narasimhaswamy, the Man-in-Lion (Simhachalam) incarnate of Vishnu. The temple architecture and the finely sculpted tower and façade are of immaculate beauty as is the long corridor flanked by sixteen exquisitely carved stone pillars; the base of each granite pillar depicts the head of a

Simhachalam Temple near Visakhapatnam

There is an interesting Puranic narrative associated with Simhachalam. The powerful demon king Hiranyakashipu was bitterly inimical to Lord Vishnu who had destroyed his brother Hiranyaksha, a notorious tormentor of all. Prahlad, the young son of Hiranyakashipu was, however, a pious devotee and would always sing in praise of Vishnu in defiance of his father's commands. Hiranyakashipu tried his best to reform Prahlad, but all his efforts were in vain. Enraged, Hiranyakashipu wanting to get rid of his disobedient son, tried to kill him in various ways. But Prahlad could not be killed with weapons, nor could he be trampled by elephants, neither destroyed in fire nor by drowning in the seas, not even upon being thrown off the mountain cliff! Each time his saviour Vishnu would protect him miraculously. In anger, Hiranyakashipu challenged Vishnu to prove his presence to him by kicking a nearby stone pillar. Vishnu, in the form of a man-lion burst out, shattering the pillar and destroying the mighty Hiranyakashipu instantaneously. The scene of the massacre of the Demon King has been depicted in sculptures carved on the temple façade.

Painting of Narasimha, incarnate of Vishnu

spirited lion. The scenic hillside of this beautiful temple, once a property of the Maharaja of Vizianagram, offers an excellent bird's eye view of the surrounding plains below.

Further south in the Godavari delta there were several ports during the seventeenth century. The Dutch had their post in Jagannathapuram and the British port was at Ingeram; both the ports faded away with the passage of time while the French port of Yanam under the control of Pondicherry merged with the Indian Republic in 1954. Narsapur on the delta of the Godavari, however, flourished as a shipyard during the sixteenth till eighteenth century. Initially Narsapur was developed by the Golconda rulers as a major shipbuilding port for the royal merchant fleet though it had been profitably utilised by the Dutch and the British. Narsapur still functions as one of the important shipbuilding centres of Andhra Pradesh. On its north-east lies the old port Kakinada also on the Godavari delta, which has now come up as a small prosperous coastal town. Both Kakinada and Machilipatnam further south, were earlier known for trading of renowned

Indian textiles and for exporting minerals, mainly bauxite. In the Krishna delta southwest of the Godavari River lies the famous port of Machilipatnam with its ancient tradition of weaving art. It was the most important trading centre of the Dutch, British and French in the seventeenth century who had all established their own ports, factories and warehouses. For the British, it was their first trading port on the Coromandel Coast. The Portuguese efforts for setting up their own post earlier in the

Hand painted design on a muslin sari from Machilipatnam

Clockwise from above: Kalamkari design; an artist at work; a Kalamkari painting

sixteenth century were foiled by the antagonised Qutabshahi rulers of Golconda. According to the Periplus (Ptolemy, AD 2), its earlier name was Masalia, and it was famous for weaving gossamer fine cotton fabrics coveted by the Europeans. From the name of its original production centre the cloth came to be known as muslin.

Machilipatnam became the largest factory of the Dutch in the entire Coromandel Coast in the seventeenth century. Golconda rulers also utilised the port for inland trading of foreign goods and re-exporting them along with other exotic Indian merchandise to the Middle East, Ceylon, Burma, Maldives and Southeast Asian countries across the Bay of Bengal. For many years the international port Machilipatnam and the nearby town of Kalahasti were celebrated trading centres for the artistry of printed textiles. In fact, for over one thousand years prior to this Machilipatnam was known to the Romans who had centres of trade to deal with the local textiles—muslin as well as exquisite dye-printed cloth known as *kalamkari* famous all over the world. The Arab traders also came to Machilipatnam in the fourteenth century via the Red Sea. Beaches in Machilipatnam are broad and pristine

An Asian pied starling at Pulicat Sanctuary in spring

with pale sands; a fishing hamlet on the outskirts of Manginapudi Beach is well known for its scenic beauty. For a long period of time, in its heyday the Machilipatnam port served as the gateway of India to trade with the outside world.

Chirala on the coast south of Machilipatnam was also known for its traditional industry of handloom weaving. During the thirteenth century Italian traveller Marco Polo visited this area; in his accounts the presence of many skilled weavers in Chirala producing the finest variety of textiles are mentioned. These expert artisans could produce a gossamer thin apparel seven yards in length that could be stored in a matchbox! *Telia rumal*, a particular type of cloth woven in dyed yarn treated with oil was a great favourite with the Arabs for its distinctive colourful design. The entire region of the Coromandel Coast was so well known for the production of varied textiles that the names of several of these popular fabrics became synonymous with the names of their respective weaving centres; for example, cloth with checkered designs were called pulicat after the name of Pulicat, a place north of Chennai. Similarly, Madras *rumal*, the name of a large handkerchief in bright colours and worn as headgear by West Indians,

Pulicat is a sanctuary for local as well as migratory water birds. Thousands of flamingoes visit every year for nesting during the winter season. Other important birds are the pelicans, painted storks, large and small cormorants, ducks of varied species, terns, herons and storks. The sanctuary is also rich in its varied wealth of reptilian as well as marine life. The lake also actively supports some commercial fisheries which in fact are destroying the ecology of the sanctuary in several ways. The International Union for Conservation

Pelicans at Pulicat Sanctuary

of Nature and Natural Resources (IUCN) has marked the Pulicat Lagoon of international importance for its unique bio-diversity . The World Wildlife Fund for Nature (WWF) also declared the lake with the sanctuary a protected area. There are several small islands within the lake. In recent years, the barrier island Sriharikota, separating the lagoon from the Bay of Bengal, has come into prominence, emerging as the centre for the Indian Space Research Organisation (ISRO) for fabricating, testing and launching rockets.

was being exported from Madras. Another popular variety, the printed chintz is basically a product of Chintadripet, south of Chirala. Machilipatnam was the first trading port of the British East India Company on the Coromandel Coast. The Company later established a big warehouse close to the Pulicat lagoon on the sea; charming handloom textiles of Nellore and Ponneri in the hinterland were traded here for export. Pulicat itself was an ancient port where the Dutch had set up a factory and warehouse mainly for dealing with Coromandel textiles. Ruins of a Dutch fort and cemetery are still visible.

Lake Pulicat falls on the common boundary of Andhra Pradesh and the state of Tamil Nadu; it is the second largest brackish water lagoon in India next to Lake Chilka along the coast of the Bay of Bengal. Located about sixty kilometres north of Chennai, a major part of the lake and forest cover is now declared the Pulicat Sanctuary. It is surrounded by southern dry tropical evergreen jungles having a large swampy dense area of a wide variety mangrove within. Three major rivers feeding the lagoon are the Arani River at the southern tip, Kalangi in the north-west and the Swarnamukhi River at the northern tip. Originally spread over a 460 square kilometre area, the lake has gradually shrunk to 360 square kilometres at present and has been shrinking further, adversely affecting the wildlife and ecology.

Andhra Pradesh, located between the Indian states of the north and the south, happens to be the confluence of diverse cultural heritages of the

Indian subcontinent, assimilating the vital elements of the country's glorious past. From the Andhra coast Indian art and culture spread to neighbouring countries across the Bay of Bengal. Being the greatest centre of Buddhism during the Mauryan rule, royal emissaries such as prince Mahendra and the princess Sanghamitra, son and daughter

Painted storks

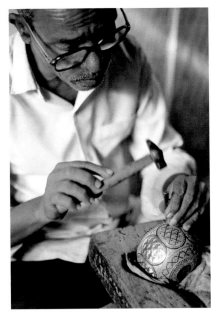 

Left: Bidri worker; Right: Kondapally toys

of Emperor Ashoka had been sent from its ports for spreading the messages of the Buddha to Sri Lanka; other missionaries went to Burma, Thailand, Indonesia and the Southeast Asian countries. Buddhism, the religion of peace and non-violence was largely accepted by all, and is still flourishing in those countries.

Andhra Pradesh is a state of many rivers, all of them flowing into the Bay of Bengal; the river valleys and deltas are not merely the rice bowls of the state, but are also vibrant centres for developing fine arts. Kuchipudi, a village on the Krishna delta, is the birthplace of the sublime musical art and dance drama presentations known the world over as the classical Indian dance called Kuchipudi; a dance academy has also been established here offering courses in various other performing arts including the popular folk performances like Bommalata or puppetry. Of the varied handcrafted artifacts of the state, exquisite *bidri* articles, charming *nirmal* paintings, exotic *kondapally* lacquer ware, *kalamkari* art and finely woven textiles have great demand in the international market.

Sunset at Kanyakumari

Tamil Nadu

From Lake Pulicat, the coastline enters Tamil Nadu, the heartland of Dravid culture, considered one of the most ancient and richest heritages of the world. The stretch of the entire shoreline from Pulicat to Kodikkarai or Point Calimere once formed the prime core of the colourful and legendary Coromandel Coast with all its glory lasting through several centuries. From the political as well as commercial point of view, this part of the east coast was once very important.

During the rule of the powerful Pallava kings of South India from the fifth to the ninth century and thereafter the rule of the Chola emperors till the twelfth century, India's worldwide international trade relationship reached its zenith. Principal commodities from India for export were spices, fine printed textiles, muslin, silk, pearls, gemstones, perfumes and bronzes for which traders from Rome, Greece, Egypt, Arabia and China would flock at the ports on the Coromandel Coast. Indian ships loaded with coveted merchandise used to sail across the seas reaching the countries in Southeast Asia and China. During the Chola regime India had an invincible naval power that ruled supreme not merely in the Bay of Bengal but far into the Indian Ocean as well. The royal Chola fleet guarded the Indian cargo ships against piracy or any sort of mercantile intimidations in foreign lands.

Through the passage of time along with trade and commerce, Indian customs and cultural heritage grew deep roots in Java, Sumatra, Bali and Cambodia, whereas the islands of Sri Lanka and Maldives became part of the south Indian Empire of the Chola dynasty. In the fifth century AD, Indian colonies in Malaya, Java, Sumatra, Borneo and Bali combined to form the Shailendra Empire. Shailendra kings were Mahayana Buddhists

Antique bronze sculpture of Nataraja

and their religion was brought to the land by the celebrated Kumar Ghose, a learned scholar and Buddhist emissary from Bengal. Inspired by him the kings built the famous temple of Goddess Tara in their kingdom. The renowned Buddhist temple of Borobudur in Java was also built by them. The temple bears testimony to the high standard of Indian architectural heritage brought to Southeast Asia. Sri Vijaya—another Hindu kingdom formed in the fourth century in southern Sumatra—had been annexed by the Shailendra Empire in the eighth century; the islands of Java and Bali thereby became the main centres of Hindu cultural heritage outside India. The most important achievement of the Cholas was subduing the powerful rulers of the Srivijay or the Shailendra Empire, who had long been interfering in India's trade with China. This part of the East Coast came into the spotlight once again during the sixteenth and seventeenth century when several European maritime powers had struggled to gain supremacy in trading rights on the eastern coast of India. In 1639 Francis Day of the British East India Company succeeded in leasing a small strip of fallow land on the beach from the Raja of Chandragiri, the ruling vassal of the Vijaynagar kingdom. On this coastal land then known as Madraspattinam, located to the north of the present day metropolis Chennai, a fortified settlement was built. Its construction began on 23 April 1640 and it was christened Fort St. George, since the date coincided with the day of St. George, the patron saint of England. Incidentally, the day was of great historic significance, as it foreshadowed the laying of the foundation stone in India of what would be the future British Empire. The nondescript, tiny settlement of Madraspattinam (also called Chennapattinam) on the sandy shore later extended, further annexing several other littoral areas; all that had merged together ultimately to emerge as the city of Madras (now Chennai). Like Kolkata, the 370-year-old Chennai is not really an ancient city but it has the distinction of having the oldest municipality of India formed in 1688. Indeed, compared with the other cities of India, Chennai with less congestion, lesser pollution and with an efficient transport system and a cultural ambience is a pleasant place to live in. Above all, Chennai is the gateway to Tamilagham, the Tamil heartland famous for its great ancient cultural heritage and its vast literary wealth.

Carved wooden figures of Lord Ganesha

Dravid or Tamil civilisation is believed to be one of the oldest in the world dating back to 3000 BC or earlier. It is supposedly linked with the origin of the Sumerian civilisation that in the remote past had spread in Euphrates Valley influencing the celebrated cultures of the ancient Assyria and Babylonia kingdoms. For their concept of Arithmetic, Astronomy, Civic and Social Mannerism as well as for Religious Perception, the Aryans are indebted in many ways to the Dravid civilisation.

Called the 'Queen of the Coromandel' the metropolis of Chennai is one of the most fascinating cities on India's eastern coast. Yet, for all its modernity and cosmopolitanism, Chennai has preserved many of its old customs and traditions.

Chennai is an extraordinary blend of the old and the new. Being the birthplace of a worldwide empire that existed till the middle of the twentieth century, Chennai has great historical significance. The old city of George Town grew around Fort St. George, the first fort of the British Empire on Indian soil. The residences of Robert Clive, Warren Hastings, Elihu Yale and Arthur Wellesly (later the Duke of Wellington), all great historic

Lord Robert Clive's residence, Fort St. George, Chennai

personalities, were located here; in its St. Mary's Church, the first Protestant church built outside Europe, where Clive and Yale had their marriages. While Clive, a leader in the Carnatic Wars and the hero of the battle of Plassey later became the Governor of Bengal, Yale was the early governor of Madras who with his amassed wealth founded the famous American university named after him. Presently the Fort area with its many interesting historic buildings houses the Assembly and Secretariat of the Tamil Nadu Government.

George Town, the heart of old Madras is the ancient part of modern Chennai with a maze of narrow, crowded streets where time seems to have stood still for centuries. In fact, it is totally another city by itself, quite different from the rest of the modern metropolis. George Town is the quarter where migrants from other parts of India had initially settled as early native traders and artisans along with the Jews, Portuguese and Armenians. Till today, there is a beautiful old church on the Armenian Street from where the first ever Armenian newspaper was published. On the eastern boundary of George Town facing the harbour, stand several grand buildings raised during the British rule, many of them as commercial houses. Most imposing amongst these is the huge red High Court building in Parry's Corner which is supposed to be the largest judicial building in the world after the Courts of London. Near the Saracenic splendour of Egmore railway station is the Government Museum and Art Gallery on the Pantheon Road. The Museum has a superb collection of rare antique bronzes of the Chola period.

Within the modern city there are numerous magnificent buildings built during the British rule. Marina, a three-kilometre-long spectacular promenade running along one of the world's largest beaches, is flanked by mansions built in the Indo-Saracenic style of architecture—the Chepauk Palace and the University. Opposite the beach is the two-centuries-old Ice House, a warehouse where ice chipped off icebergs from the Atlantic Ocean was stored by the British. Presently the House is known as Vivekananda Illam, a memorial to the great swami who sojourned here on his return from the United States. The long and spacious Marina Beach becomes lively in the afternoon when a variety of shops and stalls emerge to attract customers. Other than the shops selling seashells, eatables and soft drinks, one can often spot amusing curiosities as well, most interesting of which are an

Cardboard cutouts of Indian film stars, Marina Beach, Chennai

array of cardboard cutout figures depicting famous personalities, largely heroes from the silver screen. Here you can be photographed shaking hands with celebrities like Amitabh Bachchan or embracing Shah Rukh Khan, all against a very nominal payment!

Chennai is a city where people belonging to different religious faiths live in mutual tolerance for each other; communal disturbances are practically unknown. Rather, people actively participate in one another's religious festivities. This respect and tolerance is apparent in the peaceful co-existence of the city's many important shrines close to one another. In ancient Mylapore stands the 1,500-year-old celebrated temple of Lord Kapaleswarar (Shiva); at Triplicane is the eighth century Vashnavite shrine of Lord Parthasarathy (Vishnu); nearby is the Wallajah (Big) Mosque while close to Kapaleswarar is located the Basilica of San Thome, the most revered ancient shrine of the Catholics. Chennai is the earliest home of the Ramakrishna Mission where religious discourses as well as philosophical discussions are held.

Mylapore Temple, Chennai

*Left: A flowering cannon-ball tree (*Nagalingam*) in Guindy National Park*
Below: Night heron at the Park

A unique feature in Chennai is the wildlife sanctuary in the heart of the city. The Guindy National Park is an excellent spot for bird-watching, as well as taking a break from the urban jungle. The forest was earlier a private reserve of the British Governors, now it falls under the campus of the Indian Institute of Technology. The estuary of the Adyar River south of the city is also rich in birds and small animal life. On the river's southern bank is a vast expanse of greenery; it is the garden land of the Theosophical Society, rich in flora and some small fauna. The greatest attraction is a 400-year-old Banyan tree; under the cool, shady cover of its branches, up to 3,000 people can sit to listen to discourses of the learned theosophist celebrities.

Left: Tanjore painting
Below: Bharatnatyam classes at Kalakshetra

The crowded city markets of Chennai are dazzling treasure troves. Tamil Nadu has a rich heritage of weaving fine textiles in silk and cotton of superb quality. Almost as old and flourishing is the tradition of numerous exotic handicrafts—charming bronze and metal wares, excellent stone sculptures and wood carvings, distinctive Tanjore paintings encrusted with colourful gemstones.

Thiruvanmiyur in south Chennai is famous for Kalakshetra, the international institution of dance and music, established by Rukmini Devi Arundale, a noted scholar, celebrated dancer and exponent of the Bharatnatyam style of classical dance. Here you will find students as well as their gurus going through rhythmic steps under the trees; the singers and musicians will be seen practicing in open classrooms while skilled weavers keep busy turning out the finest traditional cottons and silks to

Chola bronze figurines from Tamil Nadu

order. Further ahead is the VGP Golden Beach, a highly entertaining place to visit on weekends. A few kilometres away on the East Coast Road (ECR) is located Cholamandalam, the unique artists' village where several talented painters, sculptors and other creative artisans live in a commune displaying their varied works of contemporary art all the year round.

The Covelong Beach further south was once the site of an ancient Dutch fort. In its place is a beach resort alongside the fishing villages. From Covelong the excellent road leads to Mahabalipuram (or Mamallapuram), fifty-nine kilometres south of Chennai. Mamallapuram is a 1,200-year-old open air amphitheatre on the vast expanse of the shore presenting an array of finely sculpted stone monuments of exquisite beauty. From the beginning of the first century AD, Mamallapuram has been a well known international sea port. It was also the second capital, after Kanchipuram, of the mighty Pallava kings ruling the south during sixth to the eighth century AD. The Pallavas were zealous architects and great builders of imposing temples and artistic structures. These spectacular creations can be seen at Mamallapuram, spread over an area of four square kilometres along the coast. Developed by the Pallava king Narasimhavarman I, the elaborately sculpted architectural pavilion begins with five finely hewn monoliths in the shape of *ratha*s or great chariots named after the five Pandava brothers of the *Mahabharata* fame. Also, there are a series of rock cut caves

Covelong Beach, one of the most popular on the Coromandel Coast

Shore Temple, Mahabalipuram

Above: Sculptors at work; Below: Mahishasura Mardini Temple sculpture

containing exquisite images of celestial figures, animals, scenes from the Puranas and depictions of everyday life. Two of the caves, or *mandapam*, contain outstanding sculptures of Mahishasura Mardini (Goddess Durga fighting with Mahishasura, the buffalo-headed demon) and of Lord Krishna protecting his subjects from Nature's fury. The most magnificent of all is an extensive bas relief done on a rocky frieze—the world's largest (27 metres x 9 metres) called 'Arjuna's Penance' (to appease God Shiva for a boon to regain the lost kingdom of the Pandavas). It is also interpreted as the descent of the celestial river Ganga from Heaven to Earth; the scene depicts the Puranic legend of the sage-prince Bhagiratha who had to propitiate Shiva for releasing Goddess Ganga, the river entangled in his matted hair, so that the freed holy river could descend on Earth to wash away and purify the mortal remains of the sixty thousand accursed ancestors of Bhagiratha.

The Pandava Rath at Mahabalipuram

This panoramic masterpiece of sculpted art depicts the engrossing scene of a lean and thin ascetic praying while standing on his one leg. He is surrounded by humans, celestial figures and animals led by several giant elephants. For its astounding vast ensemble of art and architecture Mamallapuram was awarded the status of a World Heritage Site by UNESCO

Arjuna's Penance, Mahabalipuram

in 1984. The place is also famous for its superb shore temples—two charming shrines of granite built on the shore of the Bay of Bengal, one each dedicated to Shiva and Vishnu. The twin temples, landmarks of the southern shore, had been raised by Pallava king Rajasimha in the seventh century when Mamallapuram, a flourishing international port, was his capital.

Kanchipuram, the 'Golden City', that was the principal Pallava capital, is located in the hinterland of the shoreline with its countless temples and their imposing architectural towers or *gopurams*— the soaring gateways. The most spectacular of these temples is the sprawling sixteenth century shrine of Ekambareshwara with its thousand-pillar hall and a large

Detail of a temple sculpture in Kanchipuram

Kailasnatha Temple, Kanchipuram

The Ekambareswara Temple tank

tank. However, more ancient, simple and elegant is the Kailasnatha Temple that reflects the unblemished and original style of Dravidian temple architecture dating back to the seventh century. Dedicated to Lord Shiva, the shrine has some of the best stucco sculptures of the olden days rarely found elsewhere. Kanchipuram is regarded as one of the seven holiest places of India. The city is also world famous for its traditionally woven and expensive gold threaded luxury silk saris named after the place. The weaving industry is a heritage since Pallava times when Kanchi was the dynastic capital. Over a hundred of the numerous temples that the Pallava kings raised here remain well preserved and are in use to date.

Continuing further along the East Coast Highway towards the south of Mamallapuram for another twelve kilometres is Sadraspattinam, or the small town of Sadras, which once was an important Dutch port in the early eighteenth century, but has faded away with the passage of time—only the remains of their fortifications can be seen now. The ancient habitation Arikamedu comes next where the Archaelogical Survey of India (ASI) unearthed an early Roman settlement, a trading centre exporting spices, silk and dyed muslin to Europe. Ptolemy (AD 2) in his *Periplus* mentions this place, then called Vedapuri—the City of the Vedas. Coins excavated from the site confirm the Roman and Greek presence here in the remote past. A six-hundred-year-old church in ruins is all that can be seen here.

The Union Territory of Puducherry (Pondicherry) on the shore along the Bay of Bengal, 166 kilometres south of Chennai, is a town of neatly laid out streets gleaming with white-washed buildings, flowering gardens and leisurely charms—a little bit of France and 'a window of French culture,' as Jawaharlal Nehru once remarked. Even though the French ambience is on the wane now, it is still a fascinating place. Pondicherry was formerly the capital of the French settlements in India and merged with the Indian Republic in 1954 as a Union Territory. The French settled here in 1674 and by the eighteenth century under Governor François Dupleix, Pondicherry developed as their major port. South of Pondicherry, the British East India Company had its post, one of the earliest British settlements in India, known as Fort St. David. In the latter half of the eighteenth century, the French and the British were engaged in recurring battles for seizing the suzerain power in the coveted Coromandel Coast of India. In the process, both the posts—Fort St. George and Pondicherry—changed hands several times

until the British finally won the former. The French retained their settlements at Chandernagor (Bengal), Yanam (Andhra Pradesh), Karaikal (Tamil Nadu) and Mahe (on the Malabar coast), Pondicherry remaining the administrative capital of the French colonies.

Fort St. David in old Cuddalore, the erstwhile residence of Robert Clive

Aurobindo Ashram, Puducherry

The main attraction in Pondicherry is the Aurobindo Ashram founded in 1926 by Sri Aurobindo, a great scholar, philosopher, and a patriotic revolutionary. Disillusioned with his active political life he turned to the realm of spiritualism. Through profound meditation, Sri Aurobindo perfected his system of integral yoga disseminating Indian Philosophy and civilisation to the world outside. Later, the revered Mother, a French lady named Mira Alfassa joined him in taking charge of the Ashram and administering Sri Aurobindo's ideals. Today Aurobindo Ashram is one of the world's greatest centres for meditation. The Ashram imparts spiritual education through Sri Aurobindo International University established in 1952. Aurobindo Ashram is a self contained city within the city of Pondicherry, having its own unique set up of administration and functioning. Ten kilometres northwest of the Ashram lies its new generation sister organisation, Auroville, the City of Dawn, a commune for the youth coming from all over the world to work together in peace and harmony for giving dynamic shape to the realisations of Sri Aurobindo's ideal.

On the mouth of the Pennar River, south of Pondicherry is the old shipbuilding port of Cuddalore. It was once the capital of the extensive Madras Presidency under the British East India Company. Little remains now of their fortifications (Fort St. David) that once played an important role in 1746. It then became the refuge of the British who had been ousted from their stronghold of Fort St. George at Madras because of French aggression. The old residence of Robert Clive still exists here, presently used as the Collector's bungalow. It was from here that Clive launched his successful campaign to win back Madras defeating the French forces decisively in the bitter struggle for power on India's east coast, thus laying the foundation of the future British Empire in India

Porto Novo, twenty-four kilometres away on the shoreline was an early seventeenth century settlement of the Portuguese. Its ancient name was Perangipettai (land of the foreigners). The once flourishing port has now faded and reduced to a fishing harbour. The calm and safe harbour of Porto Novo was earlier linked with several European powers trading in Southeast Asian countries. In those days it rivalled the famed port of Machilipatnam

Stone commemoration of the battlefield of Porto Novo, South of Cuddalore

A stone idol at the Chidambaram Temple

on the Andhra coast. Remnants of a Dutch cemetery, a Danish factory, an English ironworks and the ancient Portuguese fort can still be seen. The battlefield of the second Anglo-Mysore war, where the British army under General Sir Eyre Coote defeated the combined forces of Mysore's Haider Ali and the French in 1781, bears a stone commemoration.

South of Porto Novo and close to the holy temple town of Chidambaram is an extensive mangrove forest set in the maze of creeks and criss-crossing backwaters of an inter-tidal swamp. Known as Pichavaram, the marshy region has been formed by the estuaries of the two rivers Kollidam and

Nataraja Temple, Chidambaram

Vellaru draining into the Bay of Bengal. Pichavaram, a birdwatcher's paradise offers visitors a most fascinating and ecologically important natural habitat. Some of the species of the mangrove in Pichavaram have been depicted in the frieze sculpture of Chidambaram Temple suggesting that in the old days the mangrove forest existed all around.

The ancient and sacred city of Chidambaram is known for its celebrated shrine of Lord Shiva in his manifestation as the Nataraja, performing the Cosmic Dance. The sprawling temple complex containing other shrines is dominated by the Nataraja Temple that stands supreme amongst all, highlighting the unblemished Dravidian architecture of the past. The concept of a *gopuram* in the Dravidian style of temple architecture is the glorious achievement of the Chola kings who were zealous builders. Of the five elegant and most imposing structures within the complex, the *chit sabha* (mystic hall) containing the sanctum with a gilded roof is the most impressive. The *sanctum sanctorum* enshrines the bronze figure of the great Cosmic Dancer.

Chidambaram Temple elephant on its daily round

One of the soaring gopurams of Chidambaram Temple behind the sacred tank

Behind his image hangs a curtain decorated with garlands, symbolising the ethereal presence of the god who is omnipresent though invisible. For four centuries, Chidambaram was the Chola capital and the Nataraja Temple was built by King Vira Chola Raja in the tenth century AD. It is the oldest temple complex in south India. The *Abhinaya Darpana*, a treatise on dance, says:

'Whose body movements set the universe in motion
Whose speech is the source of all sounds,
Whose adornments are the moon and stars,
To that radiant Shiva, I bow.'

This unique conception of visualising god as a dancer is unparalleled in the world, though in India (in the south particularly), the idea of Shiva as Nataraja bears a special significance since time immemorial. The Lord, Master of Dances, delights the universe with ecstatic beauty of His superbly rhythmic Tandava. The Divine expression of the exalting art form in this cosmic dance thrills the spectators with awe, adoration and reverence. 'All my thoughts on the structure of the universe and its movements find a clear exposition in the concept of Lord Nataraja,' said Albert Einstein, while the great sculptor Rodin said, 'The Nataraja figure is the most perfect expression of artful movements.' A series of superb stone sculpted bas reliefs adorn the soaring high gateways of the temple; these depict the 108 *karanas* or stances as described in the *Natya Shastra*, the ancient text composed by Bharata, from which evolved the graceful classical dance form, Bharatnatyam. Chola emperor Kulottunga II built the adjacent elegant temple of Goddess Shivakami (Parvati) in the twelfth century.

Around the base of this shrine are sculptures depicting various dance poses—Lord Nataraja and dance are the eternal theme in the city of Chidambaram. All these illustrative stances are the source of inspiration, help and guidance to beginners as well as mature artists performing Bharatnatyam. During the Shivaratri festivities (February-March) every year, within the temple precincts a grand festival of dances is held and attended in overwhelming numbers.

The Kaveri River is as sacred in the South as is the holy Ganga in the North. Tamils regard the river Kaveri as their mother. The widespread alluvial Kaveri basin is the rice bowl of Tamil Nadu; the river deltas sparkle

According to legend, Lord Shiva performed the cosmic dance Rudra Tandava after humiliating some insolent sages who became proud of their yogic powers. Later, at the earnest plea from other gods and sages, Shiva agreed to perform once again in the Tillai forest of Chidambaram; but the reigning deity of the forest, Goddess Kali (the consort of Shiva) challenged him to a dance. Shiva won the contest ultimately as the goddess failed to perform certain stances befitting males only. Finally, Shiva blessed all the spectators with his Ananda Tandava and acceding to the earnest prayers of all, agreed to stay forever at his holy shrine of Chidambaram.

Rare antique bronze of Chatura Tandava Shiva (ninth to tenth century)

Sculpted dance poses on the entrance of the gopuram *of Chidambaram Temple*

with agrarian green fields of bountiful paddy and banana, tall coconut groves dominating the scene. In fact, this fertile region that was once the heartland of the vast Chola Empire happens to be the most prosperous region of the state, where every village has at least one imposing shrine. In the remote past, the large deltas of Kaveri were the sites of several flourishing ports

Metal sculpture by S. Nandhopal of Cholamondal, Chennai

which all faded away leaving behind the remnants of a few coastal towns only. South of Chidambaram, for over 300 years there was a great port of the seafaring Cholas, named Kaveripoompattinam or Poompuhar. Ancient Tamil literature as well as the early geographers and historians like Ptolemy and Pliny have described this Chola town of Poompuhar as a vital maritime port-city. It was the principal place from where Indian vessels used to sail over the seas carrying merchandise to markets abroad. Poompuhar was the port where the Chinese, Greeks and the Romans first landed for trading in India; for the Romans it was the great *Emporia Kaberis* of India overflowing with varied exotic precious items. Coins excavated at several sites on the Coromandel Coast testify the historic presence of the Mediterranean traders. It was from here too that the naval forces of the powerful Chola Empire had been sailing out to protect Indian cargo fleets on the high seas as well as to safeguard the interests of India's trading rights in countries across the Bay of Bengal. The Chola naval expeditions had not merely subjugated the opposing strength of Sri Vijaya (Shailendra Empire) in Sumatra, but had also helped in establishing the Khmer civilisation of Hindu origin and influence. Unfortunately, the glorious city of Poompuhar suffered heavy destruction caused by disastrous tidal waves over the sea; thereafter, all that was left of this 'Queen of the Chola ports' gradually went into oblivion with the passage of time, like many other ports on the Coromandel Coast.

It is believed that the main reason for Poompuhar's decay was a giant tidal wave that washed the town into the Bay of Bengal. Several onshore and offshore excavations since 1960 undertaken by the ASI have established that major remains of the 2,000-year-old port lie submerged under the sea off the Nagapattinam coast further south. The State Government, jointly with the ASI and its National Institute of Oceanography (NIO), decided to conduct further underwater explorations to discover more about the port-city of Kaveripoompattinam that finds elaborate mention in the classic Sangam literatures as well as in the various accounts of foreign historians. Today what one can see here are a few old monuments—the Dutch settlers built the Zion Church in 1701 which the British renovated in 1784 and in 1839. The church is still in excellent condition and one can appreciate the Dutch

The Danish Fort at Tranquebar

The beach at Tranquebar

architectural design of the European Renaissance. The town gateway built in 1792 displays the Danish architecture that was prevalent in those days in Europe. The Danish also built a fort here in 1620 which is the masterpiece of Danish architecture in India. It is still in perfect condition and houses an archaeological museum. The enormous and ancient bungalow of the earlier Danish governor is now the office of the Tamil Nadu Tourism Development Corporation. The imposing building of the Silappathikara Art Gallery is, however, a modern creation.

South of Poompuhar is the old town Tarangambadi (the land of surging waves) or Tranquebar. In the seventeenth century it became a Danish settlement when the rulers of Thanjavur granted the land to the maritime traders of Denmark. The Danish developed the place as an important transit port for trading in the countries of Southeast Asia. They raised Fort Dansborg along the beach and constructed the fortified small township of

Dansborg having straight roads, several fine buildings, a church, some mission houses and a cemetery. Dansborg was the first Danish town outside Denmark as well as the first Protestant Mission in India.

In collaboration with the Danish settlement of Serampore in Bengal, the missionaries of Dansborg made invaluable contributions for the development of printing in Indian languages. Tranquebar also had the earliest Tamil printing press. Though deserted by the Danes in the eighteenth century, Dansborg has survived the ravages of time with the church and mission still functioning; only the fort and the cemetery show signs of decay. Dansborg has a nice beach, but the sea here is quite rough and turbulent and has eroded several structures on the shore including the famous Gajalakshmi Temple, though sparing the beautiful image of the goddess.

Entrance to Dansborg Town in Tranquebar

Kongesnsgade (King Street), Tranquebar

Alongside the shore the high, sprawling rampart of the old Danish Fort looks out into the sea like a lone sentry. The Government of Tamil Nadu has taken up a project for the revival and restoration of the city to develop it as a tourist resort.

Within a few kilometres of Tranquebar is Karaikal, earlier a Dutch and then a French port presently under the Union Territory of Pondicherry. Karaikal is known for its Shiva temple as well as for the rare shrine dedicated to the planetary god Saturn. At Nagore is the famous Muslim Dargah of Hazrat Mian Sahab; at Nagapattinam is the ancient celebrated temple dedicated to Kayarohana, a manifestation of Lord Shiva, while Velankanni is known for its Roman Catholic St. Mary's Church. The shrines are very special, the dargah and the church in particular are thronged by the pious and the faithful belonging to all religions.

Nagapattinam, the southernmost Chola port popularly called as Nagai, was known to the Romans, the Greeks as well as the Chinese. It is believed that the famous Chinese monk and traveller Fa-Hien arrived here in the fourth century AD to begin his long and arduous pilgrimage in trail of Buddhist relics. In the tenth century Nagapattinam was the principal port of the Chola Empire. The kings had built several temples here—of these the most important is the shrine of the deity Kayarohana and his consort Nilayadakshi.

Ruins of the ancient sea wall at Tharangamvadi Beach

Several legends are associated with the shrine of Kayarohana, the most interesting one being the story of a humble fisherman named Atibhakta, a great devotee of Lord Kayarohana. The pious fisherman had made a vow to offer his first catch of the day to the god by returning the fish to the sea. One day the first catch turned out to be a golden fish, which without any hesitation, Atibhakta threw back into the sea. Overwhelmed with his honesty and devotion, the gods then revealed their presence and blessed him.

The temple complex has a small shrine dedicated to the pious Atibhakta. Nagapattinam was a fortified Portuguese settlement in the seventeenth century. The Dutch took over the settlement in 1658 developing the port further as their most important trading centre in the East Coast. However, in recent times, the tsunami of 2004 devastated the shore of Nagapattinam and salvage operations in the coastal area are still in progress.

Though away from the shoreline, the city of Thanjavur on the Kaveri basin in the hinterland deserves a special mention since it was the original capital of the vast Chola Empire for nearly four hundred years. Other than the famous Brihadeeswara Temple, Thanjavur occupied a politically important place in the history of Cholamandal (Coromandel) which once controlled the whole of south India, the island of Sri Lanka and even the Srivijaya kingdom in the Malay peninsula of Sumatra for a short period. Brihadeeswara is a magnificent and colossal shrine of Lord Shiva built by Raja Raja Chola (AD 985–1014). It was declared a World Heritage Site in 1987. The sacred place of Vedaranyam, also known as Dakshina Kailasam, is located towards the end of the Coromandel Coast. It lies amidst the salt producing zone of south Tamil Nadu. In 1930 it became the scene of the mass movement and satyagraha in line with the historic Dandi March by Mahatma Gandhi in defiance of the illegal and unfair Salt Act introduced by the ruling British.

Brihadeeswara Temple on the Kaveri basin

Egrets at Point Calimere Bird Sanctuary

Sardar Vedaratnam, the leader of the movement is highly revered by all to this day. The place is also linked with the *Ramayana*, according to which Lord Rama had taken rest here while returning from Lanka after defeating the mighty demon Ravana in the epic battle.

The stretch of Coromandel Coast after Vedaranyam ends up at Point Calimere or Kodikkarai, famous for its bird sanctuary on the Bay of Bengal. The hinterland of the lagoon, some eighteen square kilometres of tidal swamp area of brackish water, is a haven for varied aquatic avifauna comprising both resident and migratory birds. Most charming of these are the flamingoes visiting the lagoon during winter in large flocks. Estuarine dolphins and turtles are often visible at times while in the marshy lands spotted deer, black bucks, wild boars and the rare bonnet macaque can be seen.

The shoreline hereafter takes a few bends inwards within the mainland forming the Palk Strait and the Palk Bay. It is better known as the Fisheries Coast, as the livelihood of the people in the villages here revolves around fishing and the fisheries industry. Tondi on the Palk Bay is an ancient port. Gold coins of the Roman Emperors Augustus Caesar and Marcus Aurelius

Army of monkeys building a bridge to Lanka

have been unearthed on the shoreline at some spots here. Further south on the coast is Devipattinam on the Bay, which is one of the most important sites mentioned in the *Ramayana*. This small village is located fifteen kilometres away from Ramanathapuram. According to legend, when Lord Rama was proceeding for Lanka in search of his abducted wife Sita, Devi Mahishasuramardini appeared in his dream. She told Rama that all his sufferings were due to adverse planetary conjunctions. Devi directed Rama to come to Devipattinam and worship the Navagrahas (Nine Planet gods) for relief. With no shrine or image of the Navagrahas in or around Devipattinam, Rama made the images of the nine planets out of sand, while Lord Jagannatha stood guard stopping the waves from causing any disruption to Rama. Appeasing the Navagrahas and with the help of his army of Vanara Sena (monkey troops) Rama was able to build the bridge that linked Lanka to the Indian mainland. In the shallow waters of the sea near Mandapam on the Palk Strait are several small islands of interest to marine biologists. The Kurusadai Islands are surrounded by a chain of coral reefs that sustain exotic and rare marine life such as sponges, pearls, corals, starfish, sea cucumbers and a wide variety of colourful saltwater crabs.

The great temple of Rameswaram, one of the holiest Hindu pilgrimage spots and regarded as the 'Varanasi of the South', is on Pamban, a small island where the Palk Bay meets the Gulf of Mannar. The island is connected to the mainland at Mandapam by a rail-cum-road bridge. Of the four sacred *dhams* in India, Rameswaram is the only Shaivite shrine, the other three—Badrinath, Puri and Dwaraka—are all Vaishnavite temples. Being enshrined in the Puranic age by Sri Rama, incarnate of Vishnu, Lord Ramanathaswamy at Rameswaram is the reigning deity. He is one of the twelve holy *jyotirlingams* that sanctify the Indian sub-continent.

According to the *Ramayana*, it was to atone for the killing of Ravana, a Brahmin and a great devotee of Shiva, that Sri Rama worshipped Shiva in his appeasement after the great battle. Hanuman, the famed

Crashing waves at Kanyakumari—the tri-junction of seas

and devoted general of Rama was delayed in fetching Shiva from his abode in Mount Kailasa across the Himalayas; Sita being anxious about missing the auspicious moment hurriedly shaped a *lingam* of Shiva out of sand. As the rituals for enshrining were being conducted, Hanuman arrived with the *lingam* from Kailasa; thereafter, both images were worshipped and installed on the spot by Rama. In the twelfth century the monarch of Kandy in Lanka renovated the temple with stones. Since then, for over 500 years, there have been several extensions and reconstructions giving the temple its present massive shape with three great soaring *gopurams*, the tallest of which measures 126 feet. At the temple entrance, priests pour pots of water on visitors as part of a ritual—the water comes from several sacred wells of the temple, representing the holy rivers of India. For those unwilling to

get drenched, there is another queue to enter. A thirty-foot-high and four thousand-foot-long spacious corridor inside surrounds the temple complex. Its entire length is flanked by exquisitely carved stone pillars, 1,200 in all. The long corridor abounds in superb sculptures depicting varied figures of gods, animals and human beings; the ceiling is also decorated profusely with beautiful frescoes. The whole ambience is a unique representation of the excellence of Dravidian art at its pinnacle. Inside the sanctum on a golden pedestal rests the *lingam* of Lord Ramanathaswamy.

The island of Rameswaram is nearly ten kilometres wide in the west, but tapers gradually all the way towards the east until it ends up in the shallow water of sacred Dhanuskodi forty kilometres away. Other than the great temple, there are several holy places on the island, such as the Gandhamadana Hill, a fragment of the mighty Himalayas brought by Hanuman. The hillock is said to have contained medicinal plants that cured Rama and Lakshmana who were grievously hurt in the epic battle against the demon king Ravana of Lanka. The hillock bears the footprints of Rama and offers a grand spectacle of the temple city. Rameswaram is also a port from which ferry services used to ply up to Talaimannar in Sri Lanka until recently; the services have been disrupted at present due to the disturbed political situation.

Forty kilometres south of Rameswaram is Dhanuskodi where the Bay of Bengal meets the Indian Ocean. A little ahead is the Kodandaramaswamy Temple where, according to legend, Vibhishana, the brother of Ravana had surrendered to Sri Rama before the battle. The shrine of Kodandaramaswamy, also known as the Vibhishana Temple has idols of Rama, Lakshmana, Sita, Hanuman and Vibhishana. The legendary Dhanuskodi is merely two kilometres away from here. Walking through this narrow strip of path washed by small ripples of waves is highly romantic—turning your head on the right you see the Indian Ocean, while the Bay of Bengal beckons you all the time on your left. From here you can enjoy the scenic grandeur of the rising sun as well as of the glorious sunset. On a full moon evening, the sublime beauty of the rising moon together with the setting sun is a spectacular sight. Between Dhanuskodi on the tip of the Pamban Island of India and Talaimannar, a projection of the island of Sri Lanka, exist a series of reefs and sandbanks close to one another, almost linking India and Sri Lanka; this chain of shoals measuring about thirty kilometres in length is called the Adam's (Rama's) Bridge. Geo-scientists believe that these islets on the shallow sea are, in fact, great engineering feats of pre-historic human beings in their effort to link the island of Lanka with India. The earliest map calling this chain of islets Adam's Bridge was prepared by a British cartographer in 1804, probably influenced by an Islamic legend, according to which Adam, the primeval man used the bridge to reach Adam's peak in Sri Lanka, where he atoned for thousand years. However, the name Rama's Bridge (Rama Setu) was given to this chain of shoals as it is identified with the bridge built by Lord Rama's army of monkey-men. Photographic images taken from space by NASA clearly reveal the existence of some mysterious formations of shoals, seemingly a crude bridge-like link in the Palk Strait between India and Sri Lanka.

Dhanuskodi is a small fishing village that was badly devastated by a tsunami in 1964. Surprisingly, no damage was suffered by the ancient Vibhishana Temple. Fragments of the ravaged Catholic Church can still be seen here. The most important reason for which Dhanuskodi deserves to be remembered is that it was here on 26 January 1897 that the great Hindu saint and philosopher Swami Vivekananda landed after returning from his glorious missions in the continents of America and Europe. The Raja of Ramanad, accompanied by a crowd of thousands of people, had received him with a ceremonious welcome.

Around Mandapam on the mainland several fishing villages are clustered on the Fisheries Coast where Tuticorin or Thoothukodi, a sixteenth century port still flourishes, due to pearl fishing and the manufacturing of sea salt. By 1658, Dutch traders were well settled in Tuticorin which was considered to be the only harbour on this part of the Coromandel Coast where European vessels could withstand the hazards of the severe monsoon. The Dutch had built their fort in the city, then inhabited by over fifty thousand people. At Tiruchendur further south stands the temple of Murugan (Lord Kartikeya), on top of a rock overlooking the sea.

The nearby Kulasekharapatnam was once a flourishing port that has now been reduced to a small township. The ten day-long Dussehra festival in this sleepy township is however famous in the South and is celebrated with pomp and splendour, rivalling the better known Mysore Dusshera celebrations.

The splendours of the kaleidoscopic East Coast terminate at Cape Comorin or Kanyakumari, the southernmost point of the great Indian peninsula; here at Land's End is a vast expanse of waters—the tri-junction of the Bay of Bengal, the Indian Ocean and the Arabian Sea. Keenly observing the rolling waves of the blue ocean one can distinguish between their differently hued waters—the Indian Ocean looks deep blue, the Bay of Bengal is golden-green, while the Arabian Sea appears cyan in colour.

Other than the temple the most important monument of Kanyakumari is the Vivekananda Memorial, a majestic memorial raised in commemoration of the great Hindu saint and philosopher, Swami Vivekananda. On the rocky ledge jutting out of the sea stands the principal structure housing his eight-foot standing image. On 25-27 December 1892, Vivekananda had meditated on this desolate place, swimming across the distance of 300 metres on three consecutive days. Here he received divine inspiration prior to his historic visit to America to attend the Parliament of Religions held at Chicago on 11 September 1893.

Vivekananda Memorial Temple at Kanyakumari

Built in 1970 the Vivekananda Memorial is a beautiful temple in which is seen a sublime blend of various architectural heritage of India. The shrine also shelters the relics of the footprints of Devi Kanyakumari which is known as Shripada Mandapam. Mythology says that in ancient times a temple of the goddess was raised by Shri Parashurama—the incarnate of Lord Vishnu—which has since been washed away. On another rock nearby an impressive statue of the great ancient Tamil poet Thiruvalluvar has been installed. Frequent steamer services connect the mainland and the rock memorials.

Yet another important memorial built at Kanyakumari is dedicated to Mahatma Gandhi, whose mortal remains had been consigned to the seas here. The edifice raised in Odishan architectural style enshrines his image designed in such a fashion that at every year at 12 noon on 2 October, his birthday, a ray of sunlight peeps through a hole, lighting up the face of Bapuji.

Lithograph of Goddess Kanyakumari

Kanyakumari gets its name from the beautiful reigning deity of the same name. The youthful virgin goddess in her bridal finery was to be married to Lord Shiva, but instead she waits for him eternally within her shrine. As the Puranic legend goes, Kanyakumari was born out of the sacrificial fire lit by the gods for the destruction of the mighty Demon Banasura who had occupied the kingdom of heaven. Devi Kanyakumari, an incarnation of Parvati longed to marry Lord Shiva and made penances. Shiva left his mountain abode of Kailasa to proceed for the marriage; but the gods were worried that after marriage, the two would very likely be too blissfully involved in their conjugal life and forget all about the demon. Therefore, Narada the wily divine sage intercepted Shiva on the way with the pretext of celebrating the happy occasion with a musical performance. Shiva was thus delayed; the auspicious moments for marriage passed and he had to return. The virgin goddess in her bridal dress has since been waiting with a garland for Shiva. Her graceful image enshrined in the temple is adorned with a diamond nose-pin; it is said that the sparkle of the diamond would dazzle the eyes of approaching sailors making the navigation of ships difficult. That is why the sea-facing door of the temple is always kept closed.

A lighthouse, a mosque and the beautiful church located near the fishing village are added attractions in Kanyakumari. Besides its many shrines and the memorials, Kanyakumari has a unique charm. Here, at the junction of the seas one discovers oneself as part of the vast Indian humanity living through the ages, endowed with a great immortal heritage. The awe inspiring magnificence of the infinite ocean in existence since eternity is one of the noblest manifestations of a higher being; perhaps this realisation elevates the mysterious human psyche paying obeisance at the feet of Goddess Kanyakumari.

The most spectacular scenes that Kanyakumari offers are the enchanting views of the sea at sunrise and sunset; daily at dawn with the backdrop of the misty oceanscape reflecting the ruddy sky above, one finds numerous fishing boats circling the sea around the Vivekananda Memorial; as the colour of the sky gradually changes from grey to pink and golden-red, abruptly a huge fiery

Sunrise at Kanyakumari

ball of the sun rises from behind the vast oceanic stage, captivating all and rendering everything with a golden hue. However, on full moon evenings the celestial drama becomes much more enthralling; gazing intently at the western horizon nearing sundown time, one will watch spellbound as the vermillion disc of the sun slowly goes down into the Arabian Sea before taking the plunge. The sky filled with fleecy clouds suddenly becomes flushed with a crimson glow; as if that is not enough, on the east emerges the dazzling silver disc of the moon out of the dark waters of the Bay of Bengal, still veiled under a thin mist. In no time the moon grows brighter when its halo renders the dusky environs into an ethereal fairyland, infinite and divine. It is not merely a rare mystical drama but is also an unusual experience to be preserved in one's memory for ever. If for no other reason, one should endeavour to be at Kanyakumari to witness the artful performance of the two divine dramatis personae for the experience of a lifetime.